Vasiliv.

MISSISSIPPI

AFTON VILLA

St. FRANCISVILLE

NEW ORLEANS

GLENWOOD

NAPOLEONVILLE

US MAIL

President Live Oaks

LOCKPORT

TRAPPER

MORGAN CITY

So Near
and Yet So Far

BOOKS BY EMILY KIMBROUGH

OUR HEARTS WERE YOUNG AND GAY
  (*with Cornelia Otis Skinner*)

WE FOLLOWED OUR HEARTS TO HOLLYWOOD

HOW DEAR TO MY HEART

IT GIVES ME GREAT PLEASURE . . .

THE INNOCENTS FROM INDIANA

THROUGH CHARLEY'S DOOR

FORTY PLUS AND FANCY FREE

SO NEAR AND YET SO FAR

So Near
and Yet So Far

By EMILY KIMBROUGH

Drawings by Mircea Vasiliu

 Harper & Brothers
Publishers · New York

Library of Congress catalog card number: 55-8023

To Darn, Ellen, Kat, Luz and Sophy with love.

To Darn, volunteer and indefatigable note-taker, my deep gratitude, too.

So Near
and Yet So Far

Chapter One

KAT EYED OUR SURROUNDINGS WITH AN EXPRESSION ON her face that carried me back to the days when I would say to one of my children, "I know it's something new, but just taste it."

Kat was sitting on a couch in a bedroom on The Crescent, the New Orleans express, at that moment pulling out of the Pennsylvania Station in New York. She was lucky. There were four others in the group and we were all standing, because on either side of Kat were piled coats and furs ranging in bulk from capes to stoles. On the floor encircling the four standees, seventeen pieces of luggage had been deposited and counted there by four porters who had brought them.

"When Lindsay and I travel," Kat said, "we have accommodations like these for the two of us."

Lindsay is Kat's husband and an important New York banker. To common folk like me, all bankers are important. But when Kat mentions her husband, no one could feel the adjective to be redundant.

Ellen turned her head away from Kat and back again. It was a movement sufficient to allow her to see the total area of our quarters. She could not have moved much more than her head had it been necessary. But she was happy. "It will be like boarding school again," she told us.

"That's *just* what it will be," was Kat's answer, and there was no mistaking the opinion Kat held of the life she, Luz and I had shared when we wore blue serge Peter Thompson uniforms at Miss Wright's. But Luz, who even in a Peter Thompson suit had been both an athlete and a soothing influence, guaranteed that in a jiffy she would have the bags stacked so we could all sit down, and added, "Don't forget, I'm getting off at Wilmington, and then there will only be four of you."

"Four adults," Kat pointed out. She was born and grew up in Boston and is given to statistics. "In two bedrooms. Two people will have to sleep in upper berths, I suppose. I've never slept in an upper berth. I don't even know how you get there."

Our train emerged from the under-river tunnel into sunlight from the cold, clear day outside that made us blink.

"Where's my shoebag?" Sophy demanded. "I hope it's right side up."

Sophy was efficient and helpful when the five of us were together at college. Her efficiency has, if anything, sharpened over the years. She at once attacked the luggage with Luz and proposed a pitch, catch and place system for each bag. As a *modus operandi* it was probably admirable, but *in* operation it came close to being annihilating. Each time the pitcher called to the catcher, "Ready?" Ellen and I, with nowhere to go that was out of their way, swayed like willows, squatted like frogs, and begged the Amazons to "Look *out.*"

But when, with perceptible sweat, they together had lifted the last piece of luggage, a weekend case of some forty pounds, and placed it on the roof of a lavatory, stowed the coats and furs on racks above us, and in the crevices that on trains are called closets, I suppose because each has a door, we were all able to sit down. We arranged ourselves involuntarily, however, in such a way as to block off from Kat's view, for as long as possible, the luggage arrangement. It was better for her not to see, I felt, that the doorway of one bedroom into the outer corridor was sealed by means of suitcases from bottom to top, and the doorway from that bedroom into its lavatory so nearly sealed as to make entry or exit possible only on a constricted-stomach, high-breasted diagonal.

Sophy and I were together on a seat that would later extend into a lower berth for one. As a seat it accommodated two, so long as each occupant sat askew, with one hip elevated. From the hip down we were out of line also, owing to the fact that one large bag had been pushed underneath our accommodation. It had not gone under easily; its thickness had made necessary detaching the seat from its mooring catch in order to elevate it sufficiently for the bag to slide underneath. This detachment caused both occupants to teeter unexpectedly when either of us moved. Furthermore, the length of the bag exceeded the depth of the seat by at least eight inches. Our feet, therefore, did not touch the ground but hung out over the extension.

Luz was beside Kat on the long couch facing Sophy and me. Ellen sat between us in the armchair of our "bedroom suite." This was the way our travel agent had identified the space he had recommended that we occupy. A bedroom suite, he had explained, was made up of two bedrooms with a partition between folded back and the whole "thrown together." I think it was his choice of the word "thrown" that had given me a word association with space, and led me to assure my friends a bedroom suite would be spacious. In my unnatural position on the seat, I was uncomfortably aware I had had a flight of fancy.

But Ellen was happy in her chair, placed where the dividing partition between the two bedrooms was wont to be. "The chair's movable," she explained. "I was so afraid it wouldn't be. It might have been riveted to the floor the way they are on boats in case of bad weather, only, of course, on trains it would be because of curves and mountains."

Ellen in conversation frequently makes use of parentheses, and though these are given without change of inflection, her friends recognize them and subordinate them properly to her train of thought. Acquaintances, I have noticed, betray by facial expression an inner bewilderment.

Kat wanted to know, she said, why Ellen should be so unfamiliar with furnishings on trains. Kat is given to analyzing Ellen's observations, parentheses and all. "You've traveled a lot," she added.

Ellen agreed. "But," she explained, "when Lloyd was Dean

of the Law School at Madison*Wis*." (I find Ellen's parentheses contagious. Ellen, born and brought up in New York, who had previously traveled only so far West as to attend college at Bryn Mawr, Pennsylvania, so loved Madison that she invariably refers to it by her own affectionate nickname of "MadisonWis.")— "we came East in the summer on the sitter-upper, of course. With three children we couldn't possibly have afforded bedrooms and things. I always gave each of the children a sedative (under the doctor's recommendation, of course, and very mild) and I took one myself so I wouldn't worry about giving a drug to them. I had no time to explore the rest of a train to see what the other accommodations were. I did say to you, Emily, remember? I hoped in a suite there would be a chair, and that it could be pulled up to the window so I could see the country. I really gave in to you about flying *if* I could have a chair."

I acknowledged Ellen's reminder, and the responsibility for being where we were. I *had* been persuasive in my own way. Friends tell me my way is not subtle. I daresay this is so. I was born in Indiana. There are Hoosiers, perhaps, who are subtle; I have not happened to meet any of them. The ones I know are as undevious as the roads that run between our cornfields. Therefore, in my Hoosier fashion, I had persuaded, "I'll fly if the rest of you force me to, but you know how I feel about airplanes."

I doubt if there are many people with whom I have held conversation, however brief, who have not heard in the course of it my opinion of flying. My opinion of this mode of transportation is low. I am uncomfortable most of the time in a plane, and I am scared all the time. I am never relaxed. I work with the pilot, though not to his knowledge. I listen to make sure the motors are synchronizing. I have no time for the passing scene; I am watching the wings and the propellers, on the lookout for a spurt of flame or drip of oil. And I hold my breath in an effort to make myself lighter and keep the plane up. Consequently, I am tired at the end of a plane trip. But if I were asked to list the things in life that give me acute pleasure I would include eating a cold turkey drumstick, smelling leaves burning in autumn, and riding on a train; any train, anywhere, and I would put "train" at the head of the list.

So we were in a bedroom suite on The Crescent.

We saw Luz off at Wilmington, and as the train moved out leaving her waving to us on the station platform we mouthed against our window panes, like fish against the wall of an aquarium, her promise to join us in New Orleans within the week. She knew what we were saying and nodded and waved in corroboration of her pledge. Before she joined us she would have visited friends in Wilmington, motored to Lexington, Kentucky, returned home to Little Rock, Arkansas, to pick up clothes for the South. She had come from Norway less than a month before. She is something of a traveler. Furthermore, she not only flies, she is a licensed pilot. She and I do not discuss the subject.

Immediately we were beyond sight of her, Kat and Ellen requested a nap; if, Ellen said, Sophy and I did not mind keeping quiet for a little while. And if, Kat added, there is room here where two people can lie down simultaneously. "But," she conceded generously, "we can share this couch from opposite ends." She went even further. "I won't mind your feet in my face, if you don't mind mine in yours."

This generosity only served to put me immediately on the brisk defensive. As a train traveler I felt challenged. "I'll ring for the porter," I told them, "and ask him to lower the upper berth. There's no reason why you shouldn't each be perfectly comfortable."

Sophy didn't fancy sitting in the dark for an hour or so, and left for the club car where, she said, she could at least read.

The porter answered my ring promptly.

"Will you lower the upper berth?" I requested. "But don't make it up."

"You want the berths made up now?" he asked.

"I only want you to lower the upper berth," I repeated. "Take out the pillows, put covers on them, and give them to these ladies." I indicated Kat and Ellen.

The porter smiled indulgently at my friends. "You want pillows, ladies?" he repeated. "I'll get them for you right now."

I checked him a little sharply. "No," I told him, "they don't want pillows, that is, of course they do want pillows, but they also want the upper berth lowered, and the lower berth left the way it is."

The porter rubbed his hand back and forth over the top of his head, and there was a perceptible lapse before he spoke again. "Then you do want the beds made up so the ladies can retire?"

"Yes," I echoed and paused to gather strength, "the ladies *do* want to retire *but* . . ."

Perhaps I had raised my voice because Ellen put her hand on my arm and patted it, turning at the same time toward the porter, with the endearing, confiding smile that is characteristic. "We just want to take a nap," she explained, "and we don't want to undress. But of course we would be uncomfortable between the sheets, the sheets wrinkle so with clothes on, and later when we really got into bed it wouldn't be fresh, and your beds are so lovely and fresh."

Taking a key out of his pocket the porter shook his head reproachfully at me. "You didn't say you wanted just to lay down. You said 'retire.'" He looked at Kat, still seated on the couch. "Excuse me, lady," he said, "I'm afraid I'll have to disturb you."

Kat rose immediately but so did Ellen from her armchair. In that narrow space they skimmed each other like dancers in a Virginia Reel. Kat took Ellen's place. Ellen stood beside the porter looking up at him as he stepped on the couch and reached over his head to insert the key in the lock above.

"You see," Ellen began, "my friend . . ." She indicated Kat with a somewhat regal nod of the head.

The porter paused in his operations to echo it, "Likes to take a nap in the afternoon."

". . . so when my other friend," she bowed at me; the porter and I exchanged nods of acceptance of the introduction, ". . . suggested this trip I said I thought it would be wonderful; but that I would like to have a nap in the afternoon, because I've always taken one ever since I was at college. We were all at college together."

"Is that so?" The porter turned the key in the lock. He and Ellen stepped back simultaneously to allow the upper berth to be lowered into place.

I took up the narrative. I didn't want Ellen to confuse him. "The lady who got off at Wilmington is a college friend, too," I amplified. "She's going to join us later in New Orleans and another friend is going to fly from Pasadena where she lives and meet us so we'll be six. We were all at college together. That's why each of us knows what the others like."

The porter stepped up on the couch, leaning both arms across the surface of the shelf the upper berth now provided for him. He took pillows from the shelf and tossed them on the couch below.

"We're going to explore the Cajun country," Ellen took over.

"Yes'm," the porter agreed.

"You know *Evangeline?*"

The porter with a regretful shake of his head denied an acquaintanceship with any Evangeline.

"Well, my friend," indicating me, "visited that country once on a lecture tour, and she's always wanted to go back to it. So that's how we all happen to be traveling together."

During this recital Kat had been leafing through the pages of a magazine. Without looking up from it she interrupted. "Why don't you two tell him about our children and our grandchildren?" she suggested.

Ellen shook her head reprovingly at Kat, who did not see it. "I only thought," Ellen said to the porter, "*you* might be able to tell us something about the Cajun country. Do you come from New Orleans?"

"No, m'am," the porter told her regretfully. "I live in Chicago."

We held no further conversation, but Ellen watched him cover the pillows, place two of them on the couch below and arrange the other pair about to her liking, facing the window. He allotted a blanket to each, procured from the upper berth store-house, and from that same source removed a ladder which he hooked to the side of the berth.

"I'd forgotten how an upper berth works," Kat said, "it's been so long since I've seen one."

I was tempted to urge Kat to tell him about her family life, too, but thought better of it. Ellen scaled the ladder nimbly, refusing the porter's proffered assistance, and he left. The nappers settled down, but almost instantly Ellen was up again, and down the ladder, explaining as she came, "I forgot my pillow," and went to the stack of luggage piled against the door.

I trembled, but the hand of the Lord must have assisted Sophy's and Luz's in the stacking, because of all seventeen pieces Ellen's was on the top of the lesser pile that pinned the lavatory door. She could reach her bag without climbing on anything, and did, opened it without causing the pile to fall, and extracted as comfortless a baby pillow as I have ever seen, flattened down almost to the thinness of a mat that goes for protection under a table cloth. I don't know what protection it afforded Ellen, but she tucked it happily under her arm and skipped back up the ladder. Almost instantly, it seemed to me, I knew from her rhythmed breathing she was asleep.

After that everything was quiet for an hour. I lowered the shades leaving the one beside me open enough to allow me to read, or if I bent down, look out the window. But I did neither. I drifted off into a nostalgic kind of daydream, remembering how it had been when we were all at college together.

How Ellen had come from the library every day at exactly a quarter to one. We'd both had a free period at that hour, but I had always studied in my room. Every day at a quarter to one Ellen had said to me, "Will you wake me for lunch?" And fifteen minutes later, she had had to be awakened from a sound sleep.

And how Kat had awed us by her double-entry bookkeeping that had made it possible for her to ascertain, and she always did ascertain, the comparative amounts, from one month to another,

she had spent on stamps. She had employed this as a measure-
ment of the intensity of her current love affair.

And how Darn, who would join us from Pasadena, had kept a
schedule of college and extra-curricular activities for each of us
so we always went to her to find out what we were supposed to
be doing, and how she was the one who had made rounds, waking
us in the morning at whatever time each had stipulated the night
before.

And how Luz had been the most beautiful and had the most
beaux and not been able to make up her mind about any of
them, nor about practically anything.

And Sophy, living nearby, had had a car and had always
wanted to be helpful. Once, after a big May Day pageant she had
volunteered to return to the costumers all the accouterments
from the cast of *Robin Hood,* and over a bump in the heart of
Philadephia had spilled from the running board, where they sup-
posedly had been tied, the swords, wooden staffs, doublets and
hose of fifty Merry Men.

I must have dropped asleep while I was smiling happily over
this recollection.

Sophy woke us all by falling over a pile of magazines and books
Kat had dropped on the floor beside her bed. "I'm terribly sorry,"
she explained. "I was tiptoeing so as not to disturb you."

We turned on the lights and I pulled the shade beside me all
the way down. It was after six o'clock, I discovered, and dark
outside. Sophy, even after she was upright again, seemed a little
flustered. She had had a somewhat unfortunate experience.

A man sitting beside her in the club car had noticed she was
reading one of several guidebooks on Louisiana she had taken
with her from our suite. He had asked if this were her first trip to
Louisiana, and learning that it was, had begun to talk, she
assured us, most interestingly and authoritatively about the whole
Evangeline country. Furthermore, he was very attractive and she
had felt a particular satisfaction that the rest of us were not with
her. Therefore, she had accepted with pleasure his invitation to
a drink. It had been unfortunate that, at the moment the drinks

were served, the conductor had entered the car, come directly to this gentleman, asked to see his ticket and, on inspection, pointed out it was for day coach only. The passenger, if he wished to remain in the club car, could pay the difference between the coach and the Pullman fare. The gentleman turned out to be unable to pay either the difference in fare or for the drinks. To the acute interest of the other passengers in the club car, he had been hustled off. Sophy had paid for the drinks but had not stayed to sample them. She had preferred not to remain longer in the club car, and would also prefer not to re-enter it just now, nor even go to the dining car. She had aroused as much interest, she said, as she cared to incur in one evening.

Ellen, leaning over the edge of her upper berth, was all sympathy. Kat's sympathy had an overtone of complacence. Her chance acquaintances when traveling, she said, always turned out to be charming people, and frequently turned into friends; but you had to be sufficiently sophisticated to be able to judge character in the first place. I was entirely censorious. We'd all been brought up not to talk to strangers on trains, I pointed out, and the only time I'd strayed from this precept had been with a gentleman who had later been featured in the newspapers by reason of his arrest on charges of bank robbery, kidnaping, and worse. It just went to show—

Sophy interrupted me. "Where's my shoebag?" she demanded, and moved toward the luggage stacks.

At the same moment, Kat rolled out of her lower and, straightening up, rapped her head smartly against the upper. Ellen and I saw it happen. Sophy heard the crack and rushed with me to steady Kat, who was staggering a little from the impact.

"Damned bedroom *suite*," she said, feeling the top of her head, and understandably irritable. "What's in a shoebag that makes you so fussy about it?"

"Liquor," Sophy told her and went to fetch it.

The porter brought ice and pushed the upper berth back into place, but not before Kat had hit it again with the back of her

head as she stepped aside to give him room. Sophy gave her a drink first, and then supplied the rest of us.

As she extracted the ingredients, she explained why she had brought liquor in a shoebag. "I'm a conventional Philadelphian," she said (another redundant adjective). "I know there are bags made specially designed to carry these supplies. I looked at them in a shop when we were planning this trip."

Kat interrupted. "I bet they're frightfully expensive." Kat has not lived in Boston for thirty years, but remains a New Englander.

"I thought they were vulgar," was Sophy's answer. "I think it's common to carry it like that with such a purpose, if you know what I mean. I think having a drink ought to be casual and spontaneous."

No one could deny that it did look casual to see her undo the clasps of a leather valise and withdraw a bottle of gin with the strap of a sling-heel, dark-blue leather slipper around its neck. More than gin had been provided. Sophy knew and had accounted for the taste of each of us: Scotch for herself, Bourbon for Ellen, white wine and soda for me, gin and vermouth for Kat, plus cocktail shaker, strainer, mixing spoon and unbreakable glasses. And every bottle wore a garland of leather or suede.

We had dinner in our bedroom. We were a little cramped.

Chapter Two

Breakfast in bed the next morning had its precarious moments. I was in one upper, Ellen in the other. Making a hammock of myself between our two berths in order to pass cream and sugar to her, I was caught in that position when the train rounded a sharp curve. But Sophy, leaping from her lower, stood with her head and both hands on my stomach, and bolstered the sag in me until I could inch back to safety. We dressed one at a time, the others remaining berthed during the process, and the one dressed going immediately to the club car.

I was the last to join the others there. The car was empty save for our little band, and in such privacy the members were uninhibited. I had scarcely come through the door before I was aware of this.

Sophy held a guidebook and Kat a copy of *Evangeline*, and each was endeavoring to make the others pay attention to an excerpt she wished to read. But Ellen, seated across the aisle from them, had somehow acquired that morning's Atlanta *Constitution*. As I sat down beside Kat, Ellen was waving it back and forth in front of the faces of the other two, and insisting, "We can read your books any time. You must listen to this editorial on the elections by Ralph McGill. I assure you it's important, and simply wonderful."

A clergyman entered the car and the attention bidders became silent at once. Ellen put the newspaper down on a table beside her. The clergyman, sitting down at the opposite side of the table, picked it up. "Have you finished this?" he asked.

"Yes, quite finished," Ellen told him.

But at the instant of his unfolding it, Ellen leaned far across the table and spoke directly into his astonished face. "I do urge you," she said, "to read the Ralph McGill editorial. It's splendid."

"I hope," he answered after a perceptible pause for recovery from her surprise visit, "it gives a reprimand to the Democrats for their shocking behavior during the campaign."

Ellen, who is a passionate Democrat, was so stunned by this observation that she remained with her face close to his in a kind of still-pond-no-more-moving position except that her mouth dropped open.

Sophy walked over and touched her gently on the shoulder. "We're pulling into Montgomery," she said. "Shan't we go out and get a little air?"

Ellen rose without a word and we followed her in silence and in single file.

Walking the station platform in pairs, Kat and I confided to each other that the visit of each of our friends to the club car had not been the most fortunate. We delegated to ourselves the responsibility for keeping them confined to the suite as much as possible for the remainder of the trip. We conceded an excursion to the dining car for lunch immediately on our return into the train, but the rest of the day we spent in our bedroom, until about five o'clock when Kat, waking from her nap, told us she had had an invitation to cocktails with friends traveling on the same train. I remembered then having seen them with Kat at Pennsylvania Station in New York and being introduced to them.

"You're all invited," Kat told us.

But Sophy said this afterthought on Kat's part was an indication of how Kat felt about trailing three extra women with her, and that she, Sophy, didn't blame Kat one bit for such reluctance. It was as good a time as any, she added, for us to have a clear understanding that no one was to feel obligated to include the group in any invitation she might receive. "We ought to operate as independent units," she amplified. "I don't propose to be a kind of sheepherder myself, if I should happen to get asked any-where."

Ellen and I agreed positively with this statement of policy, and Kat confirmed her approval by leaping enthusiastically from her bed. She struck her head sharply on the upper berth. Sophy, nearest her, put out a steadying hand until Kat recovered from the dizziness that resulted. Actually, Sophy's arm was out-stretched almost before the crack, because by this time Kat's con-tact with the upper berth had developed into something like a *pas de deux* of the old ballet school. Whenever the upper berth had been let down and Kat approached it, night, morning or afternoon, she had hit her head on it. Not a passing graze but with a double forte sound of impact, and like a note in music it had given a cue for the one nearest Kat to extend a steadying arm. And each time Kat would grasp this as a ballerina grasps the arm of her partner. The first few times we had also given cries of commiseration and pity. Then I'd pointed out that rats in a laboratory experiment learn after only a few collisions how to avoid the obstacles in their labyrinth.

Kat had accepted the rats, continued to bump her head, and one of us, without comment, provided her with a partner.

After our social favorite had gone, Ellen, Sophy and I turned to assembling our belongings. New Orleans was not far away.

We were pulling into the station when Kat rejoined her fold. I was standing in the vestibule when Kat passed me on her way home. "Don't hurry," I told her. "I'll get porters. And that's going to take some time."

It took some time, too, for our baggage to be unloaded onto the platform. Nevertheless, my friends had not joined me when this had been accomplished, and I stepped from the train alone.

My porter indicated an isolated mass. "I put yours separate." he said.

Standing by the pile was a young couple, their attention riveted on it. As I approached the man looked up abstractedly. But when I had stopped beside the bags he emerged from the spell the sight of them had seemed to cast over him and gave me full notice. "Are you Miss Emily Kimbrough?" he asked.

This seemed also to break the spell over the young woman. She looked up, startled.

"Why, yes," I answered, "I am." And I was startled, too, at being called by name.

"I'm Jim Aldigé," he continued. "Sam Slate sent word you were coming. This is Mrs. Aldigé."

We exchanged how-do-you-do's, but Mrs. Aldigé added in a voice of wonder, "How many of you *are* there?"

"Four now," I told her, "but there will be two more. They're meeting us at the hotel."

"Six women!" Mrs. Aldigé echoed.

The echo was as good as a proclamation that the company of five other women would not be a dish of tea a Southern belle would relish. Mrs. Aldigé was extremely pretty.

Mr. Aldigé took competent charge. "I don't believe we've got room for quite all of you in our car," he said apologetically, "and your luggage." He gave a sideways glance and shook his head. "If I might get a taxi for some of you and some of the bags," he continued, "we could divide up."

My friends joined us and were introduced.

Sophy came to his rescue. "Emily," she said, "you go with Mr. and Mrs. Aldigé and take Kat with you. Ellen and I will each get a taxi, and we can manage the luggage that way."

Kat and I started to protest but Sophy forestalled us. "Go on, don't argue or we'll be here all night. Kat, you're the one to go with Emily because you've got that special message."

We accepted our assignments. When Sophy turns "general" people usually do fall into line.

In the car on the way to the hotel we talked about Sam Slate, who had been my boss at WCBS when I had had a radio program there, his official title "Head of Radio Programs," but unofficially a friend of at least one citizen in almost every town large enough to be included on a map of the United States. Mr. Aldigé added, "He's got more than one in New Orleans, and every one of them is waiting with a hearty welcome for you."

I felt the only suitable rejoinder to this would be a reciprocal toast with glass lifted high and regretted being able to reply only with a half turn and bow in his direction from my seat beside him, and a verbal assurance of gratitude. I was to become accustomed to the prevalence of a flourish of speech in that part of the country without benefit of banquet or toast.

As we entered the hotel, I stepped back for a woman at the moment entering the revolving door, and recognized Darn, our fifth member, in from Pasadena. Kat and I were astonished into inarticulate gasps of disbelief, and my introduction of the Aldigés was something less than coherent. Darn was not astonished. Pressed, she would have had to admit that the schedules of presidents and kings, or queens, can be sliced to the thinness of a few seconds, but ordinary folk cannot control a plane flight, a taxi ride from airport to hotel, allowing a rendezvous to be kept so on the dot that it takes place in a revolving door. Nevertheless, Darn would contend if you were well organized there is no reason why it shouldn't take place there.

Mr. Aldigé suggested persuasively that he and I visit the room clerk at the desk. I agreed conversation could be continued more comfortably in our own apartment than in the lobby. Kat joined us; Darn remained near the door with Mrs. Aldigé to await the arrival of Ellen and Sophy.

As we crossed the lobby, Kat explained apologetically why she was with us. "I didn't want to interfere with your arrangements and I told Sophy I wouldn't say anything to you about it, but I might as well tell you that Lindsay wanted to make sure we were well taken care of, so he sent word from New York and I'm to check at the desk. I know you thought you were getting us de luxe accommodations on the train," she added, "but I think it's just as well my husband did take over. It will be nice to be able to move around in our rooms here."

I assured her I didn't mind in the least, but explained kindly that Lindsay really needn't have troubled because Sam Slate had

Vasiliu

written asking that we receive particular care; the head of the hotel was an old friend of his.

Mr. Aldigé broke in. "I sent a note myself," he said, "that you were coming."

At the desk we waited for the room clerk to finish a telephone conversation.

Kat said she was terribly relieved I hadn't minded Lindsay's exerting his influence a little, just to take care of us. I assured her I not only didn't mind, but that there were few things I enjoyed more than a great deal of attention. "With the amount we've had," I said, "we're probably about to walk into a bower of roses and baskets of fruit."

Kat smiled happily. "You're going to adore this hotel," she told me. "I stayed here years ago. You've never seen anything like the suites, great high ceilings, lovely old furniture, and the rooms are enormous."

Mr. Aldigé had been endeavoring to attract the attention of the room clerk but he turned back to Kat, smiling with a citizen's pride to hear one of its hotels so enthusiastically remembered. "I think you're going to enjoy it," he assured us modestly. "They're certainly all on the lookout for you."

The clerk left the telephone and faced us across the counter. "Have you reservations?" he asked.

The three of us laughed spontaneously, and Mr. Aldigé spoke. "This is Miss Emily Kimbrough," he said, and also introduced Kat. "You're holding reservations for six. There's been quite a bit of correspondence about it," and he winked at us.

Sophy suddenly appeared beside us. She was a little breathless. "I hoped I'd catch you," she said. "I just wanted to tell you that before Luz left the train at Wilmington she showed me a telegram she'd written and was going to send from the station. She's an old friend of the manager's. She's been coming here for years. She wired him to be sure the red carpet was out for us, and that she'd be here herself soon to walk on it."

Mr. Aldigé laughed again. "Good Lord," he said, "not another.

The only thing left for them to do now, I guess, is to hang out flags."

During this exchange the clerk had moved a few feet away to scrutinize a sort of bulletin board on which evidently the rooms and their tenants were posted. He turned back toward us. "What did you say the name was?" he inquired.

Mr. Aldigé gave him all the names. The clerk shook his head. "Oh yes," he said suddenly, "I've got a notice here of a reservation. Just a minute."

He opened a drawer and withdrew from it a letter. I recognized my own handwriting. "Three rooms you said you wanted," and he reread the letter rapidly. "Well, you're very lucky to have them. This is Homecoming weekend as you know."

I told him I didn't know who was coming home.

The clerk took his eyes from the letter to look at me with shocked disbelief.

"Tulane University," Mr. Aldigé interposed hastily in a low tone. "Biggest game of the year tomorrow."

I apologized to the clerk and explained even more humbly. "I'm afraid I asked for just three rooms. We do need a sitting room. There are quite a few of us."

"Six," Kat said. Kat tends always to be specific.

"I understand other people have communicated with you on our behalf," I took over again, "and I'm very grateful. It was stupid of me in the first place not to have specified a suite with a sitting room."

"I don't know anything about any other communications," was the clerk's answer. "If there were any they probably came to the boss, and he's out of town. You've asked for three rooms and we've held them, and you're very lucky."

Kat interrupted. She was obviously shocked. "Why," she said, "my husband sent word especially that we were to have the very best."

Slowly and meticulously the clerk answered. "You've got three rooms. If you don't want them you've only to say so. I could fill them three times over in the next ten minutes."

Ellen, Darn and Mrs. Aldigé joined us in time to overhear this. We turned, all of us, to face Mr. Aldigé. He did not look happy. "I think you'd better take them," he advised. "The first thing in the morning I'll come round and see the assistant manager. He'll move you."

"Not a chance," the clerk assured him.

Mr. and Mrs. Aldigé left us at the elevator. They both seemed downcast, but we told them how much we had appreciated their coming to meet us, how kind it had been of them, how we were going to love the city and were sure we would be very comfortable in the hotel. They brightened a little and Mr. Aldigé said he would call us in the morning. He wanted, among other things, to arrange a date convenient for us to be the guests of the city on the Mayor's yacht for lunch and a trip up and down the river.

We all agreed that would be lovely and, as the elevator door closed between us, Kat called to him, "Tell that to the room clerk as you go by."

Our three rooms were neighbors to the elevator, two of them communicating. What they communicated was an over-all dreariness. The third possessed the same quality but kept to itself. Sophy and I took the one at the end. It was a corner room but it was also nearest the elevator. We made the acquaintance of another neighbor even while the bellboy was unlocking our door. This was a radiator in the hall just alongside us, a radiator that protested a faulty valve in a series of explosive snorts, high squeals and a steady discharge of a spiral of steam.

Darn took the middle room, Kat and Ellen shared the one to itself, beyond. Their choice, Ellen explained, was because of naps.

The temperature of our rooms must have been over eighty. It was not a remarkable idea to have the windows opened, but the bellboy vetoed it. If we did that, he said, we wouldn't get the benefit of the air conditioner.

It was my opinion that if this were benefit, the less we had of it the better off we'd be, but I allowed the bellboy to leave the room before I said so. The instant he had quitted us I opened one window but Sophy, who is a skilled mechanic, could neither open the other one blocked by the air conditioner, nor make the contraption give us any benefit. While she was struggling over it Darn came through the connecting door and asked if we had seen our closet. I told her we hadn't even begun to unpack. In this temperature such exertion might make us drop dead.

However, I went to the closet and opened the door. Sophy left her unsuccessful operations and followed me. The closet was perhaps twice as large as the ones on the train, but no more. On a pole across the center of it were exactly three wire hangers of no shape whatever that a hanger should have. The ends of each had been turned up, undoubtedly in order to hold a dress by its straps. The bar across the bottom had been elongated, probably to allow skirts to be hung across. Obviously any garment hung around or over them in their present condition would convey to its wearer a most unfortunate look of disfigurement.

"Well," I said, when we had absorbed the dismal details, "maybe we can get some other hangers from the linen room."

"Never mind the hangers now," was Sophy's answer, "let's get some ice."

While she was ordering, Ellen knocked on the door and Darn let her in. She heard Sophy on the telephone and turned back immediately. "I'll get Kat," she volunteered. "This is what she needs. She's writing a telegram to Lindsay. When I left she'd torn up three."

She returned almost immediately, followed by Kat. Kat walked past Ellen across the room, turned and looked it over. "Well," she said, "so *this* is special attention." She underlined the word "this" by a hearty smack on the top of the air conditioner with the palm of her hand, and instantly the machine came to life with a whirring sound and a rush of cold air into the room as icy and almost as strong as a winter gale. Everybody tried to turn it off, separately and all together. But in the end we got our coats, wrapped ourselves in them and closed the other window.

The ice arrived, a table was cleared, Sophy opened her shoebag and placed on the table gin, vermouth, Scotch, Bourbon, white wine, soda, cocktail shaker, strainer, unbreakable glasses. And each bottle had a shoe around its neck. Our sommelier filled each order and then lifted her glass. "Well," she said, "we're here. We're in New Orleans."

And with our coats held tightly around us we lifted our glasses. We *were* in New Orleans.

Chapter Three

IT WAS NINE O'CLOCK WHEN WE LEFT OUR ROOMS TO go to dinner. It had been close to eight when we had finally achieved our "special treatment" accommodations, so we had not taken time to tub and change. But Darn's white gloves were dazzlingly fresh. I do not remember that at a midnight fire drill in college Darn wore a pair of fresh white gloves with pajamas and bathrobe, but I can't recall seeing her without them on any occasion since.

Our intention was to dine in the hotel and go to bed immediately after so as to feel ready for an early start in the morning. Each had displayed a formidable sightseeing list gleaned from her guidebook reading.

In the elevator Ellen said she hoped the dining room would still be open.

The elevator operator answered her. "It will be open all right, but I doubt you can get a table. This is homecoming weekend and they've been pouring in since noon today. I reckon we'll be pouring most of 'em out come Sunday night." He roared with laughter at his own sally of wit and stopped the car in space, turning around to include us in his merriment.

I am not serene in an elevator. Years ago I read somewhere that, in the event of an elevator's dropping, passengers would be less likely to be killed if they jumped up to the ceiling and clung to its grating or any projection from it. This piece of first-aid information has planted in me an uncomfortable suspicion that an elevator is going to drop, and the distressing conviction that I can't make the initial jump up, much less swing like a simian. Therefore, speechless with dismay, I glared at our joker and gestured to him to return his hand to the lever. We reached the first floor safely and without further pause.

"Thank God," I said when we emerged.

His surmise about the dining room had been correct. It was open and it was also so full that a line waited in the lobby.

We dined very well in a restaurant close by the hotel. I had trout *meunière* and green salad, both delicious. Ellen and Sophy ordered as discreetly, agreeing that we would move cautiously into the gloriously rich food friends had assured us awaited us in Louisiana. But Kat, flouting such restraint, had crabmeat with a rich sauce, and when she had eaten the last morsel declared it had been succulent, and that she would now order a sweet to take away the taste of it. No one else took dessert.

Darn requested coffee from the waiter, and at the instant I had an idea that seemed to me little less than inspired. It would be fun, I thought, to walk along the French Quarter and drop in at a café. On my one previous visit to New Orleans I had been taken, I remembered, to the Old Absinthe Bar. I would lead my friends there and provide a colorful ending to our first evening. We would not go so far as to take what the name suggested. Coffee would be our selection. But if I even said Absinthe Bar aloud, Kat and Ellen, our conservative members, would, I was convinced, veto the suggestion; I was equally sure Sophy and Darn would leap at it. However, I didn't want to hurt our waiter's feelings by saying in his face we would go somewhere else.

Therefore, what I did was to shake my head violently at Darn, and follow this by a counterorder to the waiter. "No," I told him, "she doesn't want any coffee."

Both the waiter and Darn looked at me in startled surprise and Darn whispered to Ellen seated next to her, but I heard it. "Doesn't Emily approve of coffee?"

I was the one who answered. "Don't be silly. It has nothing to do with approving. Just don't order it."

The waiter interrupted with some indignation. "Our coffee is the finest you can get. And we serve both kinds, New Orleans coffee or," he shook his head in rueful acknowledgment of an alternative, "Northern coffee."

"It has nothing to do with your coffee," I assured the waiter. "I'm sure it's excellent. It's just that coffee will keep us awake and we want to get a good night's sleep. We've had a long trip today. We've come . . ."

An expression on Kat's face checked me. I was about to tell him of our trip from New York and our plans, and I think he would have been interested, but I left a sentence dangling and stopped talking.

Darn spoke. "Coffee," she said, "puts me to sleep."

"No," I repeated for want of anything better to offer.

Kat broke in impatiently. "Why on earth can't Darn have coffee if she wants it?" It is a tendency of Kat's to wish explained the reason for everything.

Resignedly, I told my idea. The response of all of them was enthusiastic tinged with irritability.

"Why on earth didn't you say so in the first place?" was the way Kat expressed it.

Even the waiter threw in a little enthusiasm. "That is a very nice thing to do. Walk through the French Quarter and stop in somewhere."

I am sometimes discouraged by my inability ever to make subtlety pay off.

When the bill came Sophy offered an idea without subtlety. "I have a suggestion," she said. "When Emily and I were on that trip to Italy"—the others knew of that trip—"I was the banker. Everybody put an equal amount of money into the pot and I paid all the bills. When the pot got low I collected again. We didn't quibble about who took orange juice and who had dessert, because in the over-all we felt it pretty much evened itself. And we avoided that humiliating restaurant scene of women dividing up their checks, sorting out the items, pushing

Vasiliu

money back and forth across the table trying to make even change, and everybody getting a little testy in the process."

Sophy's plan was accepted unanimously. She paid the bill and we left the restaurant in what is curiously known as "high feather." But we did not find the Absinthe Bar though we walked as far on Royal Street as there were lighted restaurants, and that marks a considerable distance.

I learned next day from the guidebook that the reason we had not found the Absinthe Bar was because it is not on Royal Street, but one block over, at 209 Bourbon Street. Furthermore, it is called the Old Absinthe House, not the Absinthe Bar.

We walked six blocks and then Kat and Ellen rebelled. Ellen reminded me reproachfully I had suggested a stroll, and although she had enjoyed it so far, it seemed to be turning into a trudge and she was tired. Kat agreed instantly and added crisply it seemed to her pointless to cup her hands around her face and push it against the window of an antique shop in order to try to see the interior, when next morning she could open the door and walk in. "And," she said to me, "you don't seem to know where this café is you want us to visit. Every time we come to a corner you say you're sure it's in the next block. Five corners are enough, and I don't drink coffee."

"Have fun," Ellen urged as they turned back, "but don't tell us about it until tomorrow."

Darn, Sophy and I continued down Royal Street. We passed restaurants and night clubs and at the doorway of each my companions would stop wistfully, but I would have none of it. I did concede to being a little less secretive. "Now that the others have gone," I said, "I'll tell you what I'm looking for. Either the Old Absinthe Bar or Lafitte's Forge; I may not have the names exactly right. They say the Forge was the smithy of the pirate brothers Lafitte. It was the coverup for their more profitable activities."

"For goodness' sake," Sophy broke in eagerly, "I wouldn't miss it. Let's go to both of them."

"Don't you know *where* they are?" Darn asked. Darn's is a tolerant nature, but it is put to a strain, and she says so, to understand a nature that does not know its destination, let alone how to reach it.

"I've only been here once," I told her apologetically, as we came to another corner, crossed the street and started down the next block, "and that was five years ago. I stayed right across the street from the Lafitte Forge in a place called the Lafitte Guest House, I think. I had my dog with me and the hotels here won't permit dogs. I know the Forge has big smoky beams overhead. The place is quite dark but the forge is in the center of the room open on all sides and the fire's kept going. The flames leap up and the tables all around are in darkness, maybe dim lamps on them, I'm not sure. But the place has real flavor and excellent beer."

"You're not even sure what street it's on?" Darn repeated a little pitifully.

"It's no use, Darn," Sophy told her. "I've traveled with her before. She has no sense of locality at all. That's very hard for people like you and me to understand, but it's true. I think she just sees objects without any relation to their surroundings. I've known her in Italy to walk over exactly the same route day after day and be as completely lost on Sunday as though she'd never set eye on it before, because the shop windows were closed, or the flower stand on the corner had been moved."

I broke into this laboratory dissection. "Let's go back," I suggested. "One thing I do know is that neither the Absinthe Bar nor the Lafitte Forge is here."

It was a statement that illustrated no remarkable perception. We had reached a block in which there were no lighted restaurants nor shops. There was scarcely any light at all; only a muddy glow as though the globes were dirty, on widely separated street lamps. "Tomorrow," I said, "I'll bring my guidebook."

"Don't bother," was Sophy's answer, "the rest of us will take ours."

We retraced our way without much conversation. The street was dark. There were very few people on it.

"I guess all the Homecomers are home," Darn said.

We walked briskly and close together. The air was chilly. We were glad of our wool suits and furs. And then across one more street and we were back in the lighted area again, music and people coming out as the doors of restaurants and night clubs opened. Immediately we slowed our pace and pushed back our furs a little. The air didn't seem so chilly. Darn said she would still like that coffee if it was all right with me.

"Now listen," I told my friends, "I'm going to produce something. We're not going back to the hotel with absolutely nothing to tell the others in the morning."

They as good as cheered me.

"All right," I went on, fairly giddy with pleasure at their restored confidence. "Why do we stay on this street and go back over exactly the ground we've covered? Let's strike out. Let's go left."

Had we gone a block to the right we would have been on Bourbon Street, where both the Absinthe House and Lafitte's Forge are situated, though some blocks apart. Lafitte's Forge is at 941 while the Absinthe House is not far from the aorta of New Orleans, Canal Street. Instead we went to Chartres Street, though certainly I did not look at any street sign to learn its name then. I was searching for a pleasant place where Darn could have coffee, and I saw one on the very first corner we reached when we had gone a block along the cross street. I pointed to it. "That looks attractive," I said, "and it's so well lighted I'm sure it must be all right, if you know what I mean."

My companions did, they said. However, with none too good a record so far I wanted no further recriminations because of my impulsiveness. So I urged we stand on the corner a few minutes and see what kind of people were going into the restaurant. Its windows were curtained, so that from the street we could not determine the nature of its clientele. Sophy and Darn acquiesced. In all the years of our friendship, I told them as we waited in a clump on the corner, I had never known them to be docile like this.

"I've always been willing to give you one try," was Darn's answer.

"All right," I said, "I'll show you you don't always have to be the leaders. Now look," and I indicated two customers turning at that instant into the restaurant. "One of those women is carrying a dog. It makes her look very respectable, I think. And if that restaurant *allows* dogs, then it's respectable too, I'm sure."

We waited a minute or two. The women did not come out. We crossed the street and entered the restaurant.

There were two rooms that we could see, the back one crosswise to the one in which we were standing. The back room was the darker but we could see it clearly enough to realize it was filled with tables and chairs and well filled with people. The first room had fewer tables and very few people. A bar ran the length of it on our left as we stood in the doorway, several bartenders and a few waiters leaning against the counter. One of these fairly leapt at us as after a minute's hesitation to get our bearings we started toward the back room. A little like a sheep dog circling and isolating individual members from the flock, he moved us back and over to the first table in the first room, only a few feet from the door through which we had just come off the street.

"This is a special table," the waiter said as he seated us. With the napkin that is always folded across a waiter's arm like an inverted sling, he gave a few flicks across the surface of the table as though to call our attention to its particular quality and then asked what we would like to have.

"Coffee?" Darn asked, looking at me for permission.

I laughed. Poor Darn and her coffee. It was nearly two hours since she'd made her first try for it. I was going to order a glass of beer. I didn't know what Sophy would choose and I had no opportunity to find out.

As I laughed, the waiter put his hands on the back of Darn's chair. "Ladies," he said, leaning toward us confidentially, "the coffee is wonderful in a restaurant not far from here. Best coffee in New Orleans. Come, I'll show you." He gently pulled Darn's chair toward him.

"Can't I have it here?" Darn asked.

The waiter put a hand under her arm and pushed her smoothly to her feet. "Come," he repeated, "I'll show you." With a hand still under her arm he led her to the door.

Sophy and I got up and followed automatically. It all seemed to me to be very sudden. But this was Southern courtesy beyond anything I had ever imagined. This would certainly be something to talk about when we got back to New York. I tried to visualize any waiter there deliberately taking business away from his own restaurant in order to make sure his customers had the very best the city had to offer. This one took us all the way across the sidewalk to the curb, gathered us round him and pointed in the direction of our hotel.

"You keep going on this street," he said, "until you get to the big wide one with the trolleys. That's Canal. Cross that, turn one block right . . ." and he finished his directions by giving us the name of the restaurant in which we had dined. "You'll find wonderful coffee there." He beamed at each of us. "I want you should have the best," he added.

I tipped him a dollar for such courtesy and thoughtfulness. He demurred about accepting it and this behavior I classified a Popocatepetl of improbability from a New York waiter. I pressed the dollar upon him, and when he had bowed himself back to the door and disappeared through it I said to my friends, "Could you really imagine such a thing happening in New York?"

"No," Darn answered, "nor anywhere else for that matter. I'll bet it's the first time a bouncer has ever been tipped for doing his job."

"A what?" I hadn't intended to shout but I was surprised.

Darn put a hand on my arm. "Dear," she told me, "maybe that was a respectable place that likes dogs. They certainly don't like middle-aged respectable women who order coffee. We've been bounced. Have you any other suggestions?"

"Home," was my answer.

Chapter Four

SATURDAY MORNING BEGAN WITH ELLEN'S DIFFICULTY about a soft-boiled egg. Kat reported it to us when she came into Darn's room where Darn, Sophy and I were having breakfast. I had not been in the least surprised when I got up to find that Darn was dressed, had replaced the cover over her bed, moved a table from a corner of her room to a sunny location in front of the windows, placed chairs around it, talked to her husband in Pasadena on the telephone, and written to two of her four children.

"Just like your efficiency at college," I told her. "It takes me back," and agreed enthusiastically to have breakfast at the place she had provided.

Kat, like Sophy and me, was in her dressing gown when I opened the door to her knock. "I thought I'd see what was going on here," she told us, "and what the plans are." If there's anything Kat enjoys more than her one Martini before dinner it is plans. And the wider the time space between a plan and its accomplishment, the greater her relish. I have never forgotten a January day in our sophomore year when I came into her room and found her gloating over an itinerary she had just received in a letter from her father. She had held it out to me exultingly, "Look at that," she had told me. "My family's taking me West next summer. Father sent me a copy of the tour Raymond Whitcomb has worked out. It's wonderful."

It may have been chance though I do not believe it. I firmly believe the notation on which her finger rested marked for her the excellence of the whole project.

I read where she indicated. "July sixth, Banff to . . ." I have forgotten the other place. It is what followed that has worn a deep groove in my memory. "A box lunch will be provided."

To this day I do not understand how anyone could submit to anything so inexorable as knowing in January that on the sixth of July she would eat a box lunch. And though I have thought about it over the years, I have given up trying to understand why such a contemplation should make Kat happy. I simply recognize it as a difference between us.

Darn asked hospitably if Kat and Ellen had had breakfast and offered to order some for them if they had not.

"We're getting it," Kat answered, "but it's going to take a little time. Ellen wants a three-and-a-half-minute boiled egg. Not three minutes, and not four. She's told Room Service about places she's been where the egg was 'runny' and others where an egg had been too hard. She's now explaining how her maid in New York gets them just right. At least she was when I left."

I told Kat we hadn't got down to making plans but my idea would be just to wander.

"Wander?" Kat echoed, and was obviously dismayed at so haphazard an arrangement.

I corrected myself hurriedly. "I didn't mean just wander anywhere. I mean wander in the Vieux Carré with our guidebooks."

"She means the French Quarter," Darn interjected.

"I know what she means," was Kat's rejoinder. "Remember, I'm the one who has been here before?"

"So have I," Darn answered Kat. "Remember, I was here with you? But I still call it the French Quarter. There's a special antique shop I want to visit."

Kat brightened. "That's more like it," she said. "I like an objective. I want to look for a crystal chandelier for Priscilla" (Priscilla is a married daughter living in Texas), "and a pair of girandoles for myself."

Sophy came into the conversation. "Well," she said, "of course

I haven't had your advantages. I've never been here before. But it seems reasonable to me that in a French Quarter, or whatever you want to call it, there might be French antiques."

Ellen knocked on the door and Kat let her in. "Breakfast on the way," she said to Kat, and to the rest of us, "What did you have? I've ordered a soft-boiled egg for myself but I don't feel confident about it."

I told Ellen our program and urged her and Kat to get on with their breakfast so we could start out.

Ellen seemed flustered. "Oh dear," she exclaimed, "can you give me time to telephone? You know, Bill Platt, the architect for our little house in the country."

We told her severally and together that we did know Bill Platt and the house he was building for Ellen. Ellen accepted the correction and hurried on. "Well, anyway, he wants me very much to see the Sterns' house. He built it and I hear it's absolutely beautiful, and Mrs. Stern might let us come on account of Bill, though it isn't open to the public."

Kat took Ellen's arm and pushed her toward the door. "Breakfast," she said.

We met again in Darn's room, fully dressed, each with guidebook in hand.

"I've been telephoning," Ellen apologized. "Mrs. Stern is perfectly sweet. She wants us to come out this afternoon and see her house, and what's more, she's insisted on sending her car and chauffeur to drive us all over New Orleans. She says Atkins has nothing else to do and knows every inch of the city."

I asked if Atkins were Mr. Stern.

"Oh no, dear," Ellen told me reprovingly, "that's the chauffeur. Mr. Stern's name is Edgar and he's very busy."

In the elevator I asked Ellen about her boiled egg.

"Runny," she told me. "I must explain more carefully tomorrow."

The day was sunny and cool, like the little bear's porridge, just right. Our equipment, carried one apiece, included a bulky but invaluable volume titled *Louisiana State Guide.* It is one of

the American Guide series compiled by members of the Writers'
Project in the WPA under the direction of Lyle Saxon and
Edward Dryer. It is illustrated with photographs, sketches and
maps. Its material is well organized, interestingly written and
microscopically detailed, a really admirable job, and indispensable.

Queen New Orleans, City by the River by Harnett T. Kane is
a delight to any reader and a necessity to a New Orleans tourist.
There are details here too, and meticulous accuracy, but there
are also a warmth and affection in the writing that convey a hospitable welcome from Mr. Kane. Indispensable also are *Fabulous
New Orleans* by Lyle Saxon and *Frenchmen, Desire, Good Children, and other streets of New Orleans* by John Chase.

Little pamphlet guidebooks are easy to carry and very helpful.
One is called *The Tourist in New Orleans*; another, *An Illustrated Guide to New Orleans*; a third, *Old New Orleans* by
Stanley Clisby Arthur. All of these include maps, and although
I am a shamemaking example of arrested development when it
comes to reading maps, I have pored over the other contents. We
used all the guidebooks on that bright, sunny morning, reading
aloud sometimes separately, frequently in chorus. When simultaneously, and with the pleasure of children at a discovery, we
identified a landmark we were conspicuously unlike the lady
tourists I passed one day in the Louvre in Paris at the moment one
said to her companions, "Now I'll read and you look. We'll get
through much faster that way."

We had no desire to get through fast and we all wanted to read
and look. I daresay we were conspicuous, too; five middle-aged
women, strolling, gaping and reading aloud. But happily we were
of one opinion that when you are a sightseer it is a silly affectation
to conceal the fact that you are sightseeing.

For a little way on Royal Street from Canal, the prospect does
not please. There are tawdry little souvenir shops, garishly lighted
and crowded together. But presently the treasures are revealed
if you look for them. For over twenty years on Easter morning
I have secreted the loot for an Easter egg hunt for my children,
and now in addition to my children, their children. And I have

discovered that the greatest pleasure for them is loot a cut above the colored Easter eggs, put in places hardest to find. The Vieux Carré is a tantalizing Easter egg hunt, and there is more loot than you can carry home in your memory.

Just by looking on them you will not discover that sidewalks there are called *banquettes*. But the guidebook will tell you the original raised planks that were the first paths for the fashionable citizens are still called by the French name. You must look carefully for house numbers, we learned that morning, because the numbers are repeated in the guidebooks to identify each building and its background. Number 121, for instance, once housed a remarkable assortment of tenants; Spanish agents planned Central American revolutions there, and Dr. Anton Marci occupied an office. He was Napoleon's physician on St. Helena. The famous death mask of Napoleon used to be exhibited there but it, or its copy, is now in the Cabildo.

If it were not for the skill and courtesy of New Orleans drivers, our trip and our lives could have ended that morning. Guidebooks in hand absorbing our attention, we stepped heedlessly off curbs, wandered to the middle of the street and stopped there in order to have an unrestricted view of the exquisite iron balconies above our heads. But not one of us was grazed, though we ambled back and forth across the street without plan or warning. How could we bother about cars when at 415 Royal we must back to the middle of the street and look up, to untangle from the intricate lacework of the balcony the monogram of the original owner, Adrian Rouquette? From this spot we also saw that the first floor was occupied by a perfume shop called René. We promptly tucked our guidebooks under our arms, crossed the street once more, entered the shop and were immediately on one of the two main avenues of particular delight to tourists: the first, sightseeing, the second, shopping.

Monsieur René is as French as a resident of Paris although his family has been listed on the records of Louisiana citizens for many generations. He himself has never been to France, but he speaks very little English. Meeting him was our introduction to

the people, apart from the places, we had come to Louisiana to find: descendants of the French pioneers who, emigrating from their homeland, had chosen to subdue and live among, God knows why, the fever-ridden jungle forests, swamps, bayous and rivers that characterized Louisiana in those days. The Cajuns were French too, but settlers in Louisiana by way of far-off Acadia in Nova Scotia, driven from there by the British early in the eighteenth century. The word "Cajun" is a corruption of "Acadian." This was what we had been reading about. This was why we had brought copies of *Evangeline*. And we were face to face with Monsieur René, a fourth-generation American at least, who spoke almost no English.

The fact that Madame René spoke English, and I think very little French, made her no whit more American than he. But as husband and wife they provided to our pleasure an ingredient of what makes Louisiana unlike any other state in the country. Their products pleased us, too. The basic oils for his perfumes, Monsieur René told us, come from France, but he blends the scents himself according to formulae handed down to him from his forebears.

I found his French easy to understand; I'm not sure he was equally happy with mine. Madame told us they have customers from all parts of the country who annually reorder their favorite blend. My name has now been added to their list.

I came away with "Bayou Sauvage." I would have chosen it for the name alone but the fragrance was just to my liking. I also took with me "Toi et Moi," "Nuit et Jour" and "Jasmine," as gifts for friends. They are all inexpensive. I do not wonder that travelers who have discovered them reorder.

We came out again and "picked up," as the old automobile guidebooks used to say, our sightseeing. We progressed only as far as 417 Royal Street, when Sophy read that this was one of the most interesting buildings in the Vieux Carré. "Notice round windows on third floor."

And so to the accompaniment of screaming automobile brakes, we were in the middle of the street again in order to see the windows. The building was once a bank, Sophy read, and later the Morphy family lived in it. Paul Morphy, we had already learned, because there are many references to him, was the world's greatest chess player.

"You can go in," Sophy read. "The court is lovely, now a fashionable restaurant. Interior worth inspection. Double stairway is a thing of beauty, admired by visiting architects."

It was also admired by our group of visitors, but we were not yet ready for lunch and went on up the street. We crossed to the other side at 520 to see the courtyard of this beautiful building that was once the residence of a French wine merchant. Pure aesthetes, I'm sure, would have been oblivious to everything but the exquisite ironwork tracery on the third-story balcony there; and the graceful lines of the balconies themselves. Thank goodness our group was not so pure. Across our faces as we stood gaping up was wafted a warm smell of something that was cooking, sweet and pungent. Simultaneously we sniffed, flared our nostrils and followed them to a tiny shop tucked in a far corner of the courtyard. There were souvenirs for sale, but there were also small fresh pralines cooking in front of our very eyes. The owner, saying this was her little shop and that she hoped we liked it, slid five pralines from the stove to a plate and offered one to each of us.

We were right back to buying again.

On our short and wayward journey down Royal Street we had already passed close to a dozen shops advertising, each one, the best pralines in New Orleans. But not one of the shops had wafted across our noses the smell of hot, fresh cooking pralines. That one whiff and we were goners.

Sophy laid on the palm of her hand a two-pound box and extended the other palm toward us like the Goddess of Justice with her scales. "Fun, or our figures?" she inquired.

The only answer she got was a derisive jeer from the group and an admonition from me not to be stingy.

"I'd like to order some to be sent," Kat put in, and explained to us she thought her children and her grandchildren would enjoy them. "But one-pound boxes are enough," she cautioned the lady on the other side of the counter. Kat does not believe in being excessive. "And," she turned back to us, "if I'm sending Priscilla a crystal chandelier, I'm not going to include a box of pralines."

I finished my orders and, while the others were completing theirs, wandered back into the courtyard. There was a stone bench on the side opposite the little shop and I sat down. It made cold sitting, but the upper part of me was in the sun and I had a lovely view, without exertion, of the ironwork above.

A colored maid, in uniform with a bandanna around her head, came out of a door on the balcony. She was singing and walked with a slow, swinging step, disappearing at last through another doorway farther down. Perhaps people live in apartments above this courtyard, but I was too contentedly lethargic to go back to the shop and inquire.

A little colored boy came into the courtyard from the street. He was whistling and carried shoeshine equipment. I hailed him and asked him to polish my shoes. I wanted to talk to him, and found him gay, intelligent, altogether charming. He told me he was eleven years old and, though he lived some distance away, worked in the Quarter in after-school hours and all day Saturday and Sunday. I told him the guidebook said there were guard-screens to be seen there, designed to keep marauders from passing from one balcony to another.

Darn came out of the shop while we were having this conversation and called she was going out to the street and would pick us up there.

The little boy told me he had never heard of the screens, but added politely he hoped I would find them.

The others came out soon after Darn. Kat and Ellen went ahead to join her. Sophy sat down by me and asked the little boy to shine her shoes when he had finished with mine. I got up when he had finished and told Sophy I was going to find the others and we would wait for her. Sophy followed me a few feet, saying to the little boy she'd be back. When we were out of his earshot she stopped me. "Now look," she said, "I don't really care what else you accumulate on this trip, but I beg of you not to try to take that little boy home with you."

Perspicacity is undoubtedly a splendid quality but I could wish Sophy were not blessed with it. "I wouldn't think of such a thing," I said. "He did tell me he was longing to come North and get an education there. He's very intelligent. You can tell that in a minute."

"I knew it," was Sophy's answer. "Remember that little Indian boy you very nearly brought back from Oklahoma? Remember the man in Arezzo, who wanted you to get him back to Chicago, and the little Italian boy in the market at Perugia?"

I had intended to wait in the street until Sophy came out lest she ask embarrassing questions, and then slip back only to secure the child's name and address. But it is difficult to carry out one's impulses when a solid block of logic is standing in the way.

I found Kat and Ellen across the street with Darn. Actually I could see through its window that Kat was inside an antique shop with Darn. As I stood at the entrance to the courtyard looking up and down the street for them, Ellen was the first I caught sight of. Had we been playing "the game" I would have guessed immediately that she was giving an interpretation of a bird dog. She moved quickly in one direction along the street, pausing now and then to look up, probably at ironwork, and again into shop windows. I doubt that she actually was sniffing but she gave the appearance of "pointing." Then she went the same distance in the opposite direction repeating her procedure. She went out into the street, looked up at the building on her side, cast a quick glance across the street but did not recognize me, made a wide arc and came back on the sidewalk a little farther away than her first point of departure. I watched with interest while she repeated this coverage. I was reluctant to interrupt it, but on the round into the street while doing the second lap she caught sight of me and called, "We're over here. I've been looking for you."

When I had joined her on the opposite sidewalk she amplified.

"Kat and Darn are in an antique shop. I said I'd watch for you. But just watching seemed such a waste of time, I thought I could *look*, too. I found some perfectly darling shops and what heavenly ironwork."

She pointed up, and I, agreeing with her, had a sudden start of discovery. "There are the guardscreens I was looking for," I explained. "I thought they were inside the court."

They are on the street side at either end of the balcony there, and quite sinister. The screens are actually like the bars of an iron fence except that the upper end of each is curved down and ends in a sharp spike. I had not realized it was the outer balcony that had been protected. But I saw that the buildings are so close together without this barrier one could climb easily over the rail of one balcony and be on that of the adjoining residence.

Darn and Kat came out of the shop accompanied by an attractive-looking woman who was talking with them. Joining us, she continued. "I've just been telling your friends," she said, "you ought to telephone the Louise S. McGehee School for Girls. The school sponsors a tour of the old homes in the Garden District. That's our rival, you know, for sections of New Orleans to visit. It's where the beautiful old homes are, mostly Greek Revival."

Instantly I became a sister pointer to Ellen, stiffening in happy anticipation, because any building in the style of the Greek Revival is one of my favorite things in this country to see.

"If you have a minute," our impromptu guide told us, "I'll be happy to call up the school for you and find out more about it."

Sophy came from across the street. We explained to her what was going on, and she followed us into the shop.

During the telephoning, Darn urged us to look about. "This is Casey, Casey and Butts," she said. "It's the place I wanted to find again. They specialize in English antiques."

Their pieces were beautiful, and from the look in Darn's eyes I knew that before we left New Orleans some of them would be on their way to her house. But we got her away on this first visit with only the information about the Garden District, because, as

I pointed out, she could not buy a piece of furniture with the lack of selectivity that had been possible when ordering pralines.

"Speaking of pralines," I added, "I'm frightfully hungry. Don't you think we could have lunch now?"

My suggestions are not always acceptable to a group. This one was met with enthusiastic approval.

We took with us the address of the school, 2343 Prytania Street, and the knowledge that visits to the old houses of the New Orleans Garden District are possible by arrangement from October through May. It is a school project for the benefit of the school itself and part of the proceeds from the admission fees are also used for the preservation and upkeep of such of the houses as could otherwise not be maintained. Not all of the homes are open at all times. Therefore, the school must be telephoned for the list of those available at the moment.

We lunched at the Court of the Two Sisters at 613 Royal Street. I am too simple of mind and taste to understand why the identification of a place as "touristy" is considered by some sophisticates to be derogatory. When I am a tourist I like to go to places where other tourists go. I do not mean by that that I have enjoyment from spots that are crowded. I happen not to like crowds. But I follow the assumption that a choice of tourists is based on something about the place that pleases them. Therefore, in all probability, it will please me. The Court of the Two Sisters pleased all of us.

A broad enclosed flagstone passage leads from the street to the courtyard proper. After the brightness of the street the passageway seemed dark at first, but standing in the archway that marks its entrance, we saw that a roaring fire in a tremendous fireplace on the left was sending out the glow that was not sunlight. We passed, on our right as we moved toward the courtyard, a bar and then a beautiful broad sweeping staircase. And on the wall to our left saw the *specialités de la maison* written large on a blackboard, and paused to make note of them. Then we were in the courtyard proper, large enough for a coach and four to turn in. It runs straight through the block to Bourbon Street where there is also an entrance. The court is enclosed by a high wall, vine covered, and there are trees for shade.

We selected a table partly under one of these because the day was too cool for total shade, but too bright for sitting in the full sun. After we had ordered we read from a guidebook that the Court of the Two Sisters was built in 1832 by Zenon Cazelier when he was President of the Banque d'Orleans, and had been one of the great residences of the city, but that it had gained its present name from the fact that from 1886 to 1906, two sisters, Emma and Bertha Camors, had conducted a "fancy and variety store" there. I am not halfhearted in my observance of tourist customs. When traveling, I buy picture post cards, I carry a camera and a guidebook, and that day in the dappled sunlight of the Two Sisters courtyard, I persuaded my friends to have a group photograph made by a young woman whom I had seen moving from table to table and soliciting this privilege from its occupants. The finished photographs were presented to us at the end of our meal: one of the group, and in addition individual match cases each carrying the head of one of us pasted on the inside of the cover. The acquiescence of my friends went only so far as to their submitting to being snapped; I had to pay for the lot. The likenesses were good but startlingly dappled by sunlight.

We lunched well and lingered over our coffee waiting for the photographs to be finished. Ellen and Kat took this opportunity to visit the Maison de Ville because they discovered a gateway through the wall on one side of our courtyard that led directly into its garden, though the proper entrance is on Toulouse Street. A friend of Kat's and mine had written us about this little place in the Quarter, urging we stay there. But at the time we had felt so much trouble had been taken about our reservations at the hotel we had not wanted to change.

The two explorers came back starry-eyed. It was completely charming, they reported; small, beautifully furnished, intimate, and its own garden a delight. Ellen concluded ruefully, "But I think we must be practical. I don't believe the switchboard is big enough."

I am not often baffled by Ellen's conclusions. This one, however, I found too cloudy to penetrate. "Why does a switchboard have to be big?" I asked.

Ellen explained. "Well, dear, you know Kat and Darn and I have husbands, and Sophy has her Urban League and you'll have people calling probably wanting to show you things. I think it's too much for one little switchboard and one little operator and nobody there at night at all."

Sophy said no matter who had a husband, or whatever, we all had seventeen pieces of luggage, and that was too much to move. She added darkly, "And you know who'll be doing the moving. The three of you will be drifting around sightseeing and Darn and I will be left heaving the bags."

We decided to stay where we were.

We had just got home when Atkins, Mrs. Stern's chauffeur, came for us. He drove us first to the water front past the old market and Jackson Square, and we paused to identify from the guidebook 823 Decatur Street where the famous restaurant Madame Bégue's had been; that restaurant where one sat down to breakfast at eleven and rose at three in the afternoon. Her successor calls the restaurant now Tujagues, and Darn made a note that we must visit it.

We realized almost immediately we had no need of the guidebooks. Atkins knew as much as they and told us more than was contained in their pages: not only the identity of the buildings and the houses we passed, but the stories of their early and present-day occupants. He drove slowly, stopped, told us a story, moved on again. I asked if he'd always lived in New Orleans and he answered with a list of the places in which he'd stayed long enough to be counted a resident. It was a staggering list that pretty well covered the country. I wanted to know which city he'd liked best.

I was sitting beside him and he took his eyes from the road to look at me for a long moment with respectful astonishment. "Why," he said, "New Orleans . . . There's not a city in the world so beautiful as New Orleans." He paused a moment. "And it's my home," he added.

This was the only unqualified statement Atkins gave us. When, having closed the guidebook, Kat asked the name of a handsome building we were at the moment passing, Atkins answered, "They tell me it used to be the old United States Mint. But now for n'instance, you *could* say it's the Coast Guard Headquarters."

A few minutes later Darn, who always likes her bearings definitely set, asked him in what direction we were heading. His answer was, "M'am, we're going what you *might* call west."

We turned into the Esplanade and along that beautiful, wide street we traveled at a pace an Austrian had once described to me. "I moved," he had said, "almost hardly." We moved "almost hardly" along the Esplanade, because there was so much of beauty to see and there were so many times when I had to get out of the car to photograph an exquisite balcony or, again, a little rosy pink brick building, separated from a handsome house by a walled garden. The little building had been originally the slaves' quarters, Atkins told me.

However, we did reach the end of the Esplanade and after that picked up speed to reach the shore of Lake Pontchartrain. The houses here are new, in a recent residential development, but the lake is not. There were a few sailboats on its bright blue water, and more in the harbor of the yacht club that we passed. We detoured from the highway into the Metairie Cemetery, and there we were lost for half an hour. We didn't mean to be; we were not dreaming our way among the tombstones. Atkins simply couldn't find the way out. He was disgruntled. He was also mortified, he said, though we assured him we were enjoying ourselves.

This is not one of the old cemeteries, but it follows the style of burial on top of the ground that was once a necessity, because the land was so little above, and so frequently below water. Like everything else in New Orleans, Metairie Cemetery has a story. Its land had once been the Metairie Race Course. The story goes that a gentleman who wished to join the club of which the track was part was refused membership. Enraged, he swore he would put an end to the club and the track, and did. In 1870 he purchased the land, track included, and promptly turned it into a graveyard. As a final and permanent triumph, he elected himself its charter member. His was the first interment there.

It was nearly five o'clock when Atkins unexpectedly came upon the exit and drove us within a few minutes to the Sterns' house. Mrs. Stern was waiting for us. Her charm and warmth made us feel at home immediately. But seeing her at bay in the teeth of an invasion by five total strangers, I admired most of all her serenity. We talked for over an hour, walking through the beautiful house and out into the exquisite formal garden, before I discovered that Mrs. Stern and I had been together at Miss Faulkner's School in Chicago when Mrs. Stern was Edith Rosenwald. I felt deeply ashamed of my dimness of wit until some hours later back at the hotel I derived comfort from the sudden realization that she had not remembered me either. However, I had no sooner reassured myself about this shortcoming of mine than Kat presented me with another. When the group had been assembled in Sophy's and my room by our sommelier, and she had emptied her shoebag and was mixing the contents, Kat took a stand.

"I have something to say," she began, "and I think it's just as well to say it right off, in the beginning of our trip." She turned to me. "Would you mind telling me, Emily," she asked, "why, when Mrs. Stern asked us if we'd like a cocktail, you spoke up for all of us and said, 'Oh, no thank you, it's terribly kind of you but we must get back'?"

I started to explain but she silenced me.

"Now wait," she continued. "That would have been all right, though I don't know why we couldn't have had one of Mrs. Stern's cocktails. I don't suppose she makes them from a shoebag, but that wouldn't come out in the taste. Anyway, I wouldn't have minded so much your refusing for all of us if we had left. But did we? No. We sat on for at least half an hour, talking, and I saw a maid in the hall carrying a tray of canapés. So they must have been expecting us to stay. Very wasteful, I call it."

I was all apology. I'd thought we were going, I explained, and then I made the mistake of saying I'd tried to expedite our getting away because I'd thought Kat and Ellen would want their naps. This succeeded only in miffing Ellen as well as Kat; they became a vehement chorus asserting they didn't have to have naps, they only took them when there was time and nothing else to do. Even Darn came into it unexpectedly, protesting, though mildly, that she had been getting the most valuable information from Mrs. Stern about the best antique shops in New Orleans. That Mrs. Stern was truly an authority and they'd been having a wonderful time.

And then Sophy, handing me my glass of white wine and soda, shook her head reproachfully. "Mrs. Stern had been telling me about oyster bars," she said, "places where you stand up at a counter to eat raw oysters opened for you while you wait, and some out-of-the-way restaurants to try. But you didn't wait to let me hear about all of them."

I felt an uneasy suspicion that at the moment I was not universally loved. I offered to go downstairs and talk to the clerk at the desk about keeping one room for surplus bags and belongings while we were away from New Orleans. Nobody said, "Oh, don't bother." So I left.

The clerk was considerably warmer toward me than my friends had been, and startlingly more cordial than he had been at our arrival. We not only could keep one room, he assured me, but wouldn't we like to be moved into a suite? They had a lovely one; the manager, he added, had just got home and had found some communications about us. I told him I would confer with my friends and went back to join them.

But as I stepped into the elevator its only other passenger, braced determinedly against the wall of the cage, stretched out an arm and to my considerable surprise drew me into a warm embrace. In his other hand he held a highball and pressed that to me, too. "Let's celebrate Homecoming together," he invited inarticulately, and added loudly, "Hurrah for Tulane!"

That burst of loyal sentiment overtaxed his balance and he slid to the floor, releasing me. I am a craven in the vicinity of intoxication. Such close proximity to it sent me into an idiotic panic. I muttered something foolish about having forgotten an errand and scuttled from the elevator, saying to the operator as I passed, "Shut the door quick."

I waited around the corner, peeking out from time to time until I saw the other of the two cars descend and unload its passengers, and then I shot into it, urging the operator not to wait for other passengers, that I was in a great hurry. Once inside home sanctuary I did not wait to take its temperature. "We have to have dinner up here," I said. "The Homecomers are drunk, and I won't go downstairs again while they're milling around. The game is just over, I guess, and they're coming back here by the hundreds."

I am grateful to that drunk. He brought my friends back to me, soothing, sympathetic and indulgent. We had dinner in Darn's room.

About nine o'clock Mr. and Mrs. Crager sent word they were waiting for us in the lobby. When we went down to meet them the Homecomers had dispersed. Tess Crager owns and operates the Basement Book Shop and Library that is at 7221 Zimple Street, out by the university, and one of the most delightful and provocative-to-browsing book shops I know. The reason the shop has such charm is Tess Crager. She is warm of heart and sharp of wit. And she happens to love books. Her husband is a publisher. They took us to the Richard Grahams'. Robert Tallant was there. I had hoped to meet him in New Orleans because I knew and had deeply enjoyed some of his books. I learned that Alice Walworth Graham's new book was just out. So we talked shop, but there was general talk too. It was the nicest kind of an evening; the New Orleans folk eager to tell us places in the Cajun country to see, houses along the Mississippi to visit, and all the information interspersed with rich anecdote.

The Cragers returned us to the hotel and, as we said good night, begged us to let them help in any way possible—tell them people we'd like to meet, places we'd like to see not open to the public. Would we call on them and in the meantime they would call us with other ideas that might come to their minds.

Upstairs as we separated for our rooms I repeated happily, "Wasn't that a good party? And did you ever meet more outgoing, hospitable people?"

Kat put a hand on my arm. "Darling," she said, "it was divine. Only why did you stay so long? Nobody could go ahead of us because the party was *for* us; but when it got so late everybody wanted to break it up except you. You ought to know when to go. We should have left an hour ago."

Chapter Five

ELLEN AND DARN SAID KAT AND SOPHY TIMED THEIR
departure from the Sunday-morning service in the cathedral to
avoid the collection. The two errants called this a libelous accu-
sation. They protested they'd gone into the cathedral because it
was beautiful, but not being Catholics had not known at what
moment the collection would be taken and, seeing other people
coming and going, had themselves returned to the sunshine and
the sights out of doors. Sophy volunteered to return and drop
an offering in the alms box but Kat pronounced this an admission
of guilt, adding that she was arguing from principle not expendi-
ture. They were discussing the matter when I joined them at half
past twelve outside Brennan's French Restaurant on the corner of
Bourbon and Bienville Streets.

"Mike Brennan," Mr. Aldigé had said, "runs one of the best
French restaurants in New Orleans. Their specialty is Sunday
brunch and everybody goes. Half past twelve is the fashionable
time and people *do—*"

I'd reassured him, "I know, people *do* wear their Sunday-go-
to-lunch clothes. I promise you we won't wear our sightseeing
low heels and we won't bring our guidebooks."

At twelve thirty precisely, we tossed back our furs to a stylish
draping across the shoulders, and Darn, whose white gloves seem
mysteriously always whiter than anyone else's, pushed open Mr.
Brennan's door. A table had been reserved for us. Several waiters
hovered round us. We were no sooner seated than one of them
said, "Miss Brennan wants to know when you come. I go tell her."

She came immediately from the kitchen and as she approached I thought what friendliness and humor were in her attractive Irish face. She was all that her looks promised. "Mr. Aldigé said you'd come," she told us as we shook hands all around, "and my father and I are so happy to have you here. My brother's not in at the moment. He'll be here soon. It's all in the family. Now what will you have to drink to start off with? And then you must have the finest French meal."

There was a wee trace of "the foinest" in her speech and we warmed to it, but we were startled into little cries of apology and dismay by her suggestion.

"Oh, mercy," I said, "I'm afraid we couldn't drink anything in the middle of the day. We never do."

"Come now," was our hostess's answer. "Surely you can't call Sunday brunch the middle of the day. Why, for us here it's just the natural follow-up of a Saturday night."

Remembering that by choice we had drunk ginger ale or plain soda at the Grahams' the night before, I felt our Saturday-night roistering was not up to New Orleans standard. Evidently Darn shared my sense of deficiency and was ashamed of it, because she announced suddenly, "I'll have a Zackery."

As a gesture it was worthy of D'Artagnan himself, but as a means of raising us to a level of equal sophistication with the New Orleans haute monde, it was lamentable. The name at which she had aimed turned out to be Sazerac, a cocktail for which the city is famous. Miss Brennan pointed this out with the utmost tact, but made no further protest when we said we thought perhaps we'd just order food.

At a signal the waiters closed in on us and presented each with a menu of a size that totally extinguished, as we held them up, each head behind it. This was the choice offered us for that Sunday-morning breakfast: (See the following pages.)

In the happy lethargy that crept over us as we ate our own food and sampled one another's selections, we made no protest over a bottle of champagne brought to us in a bucket of ice with the compliments of the Brennan family. On the contrary. But as

Come as late as Midnight for Supper

Absinthe Frappe .65

Absinthe Drip .65

Absinthe Suissesse .75

Milk Punch .75

New Orleans Gin Fizz .75

Ojen Cocktail .75

COMBINATIONS

Grilled Grapefruit with Kirsch   1.75
Omelette with Fresh Mushrooms
Cafe au lait

Cantaloupe and Honeydew Melon Balls   5.40
Lamb Chops Mirabeau
Brabant Potatoes
Cafe au lait

Sliced Peaches with Cream   2.00
Grilled Ham Steak, Fried Bananas
Cafe au lait

Baked Apple with Cream   3.90
Breakfast Cut Sirloin Bearnaise
Brabant Potatoes
Cafe au lait

Fresh Fruit Compote   2.50
Eggs Sardou
Cafe au lait

Creole Cream Cheese   2.30
Chicken Liver Omelette
Cafe au lait

Bananas with Cream   2.30
Eggs a la Turk
Cafe au lait

Stewed Prunes   3.50
Eggs Benedict
Fresh Fruit aux Kirsch Flambe
Cafe au lait

Strawberries with Cream   7.00
Egg St. Denis
Filet Mignon Mirabeau
Crepes Suzette
Cafe au lait

Cognac in Heated Sniffer   1.00

BRENNAN'S recommends with Breakfast,

LIGHT PINK WINES AND CHAMPAGNE

California's Best Rose Wine   Bottle 3.00   Half 1.50

French Tavel   Bottle 6.00   Half 3.25

American Champagne: 1/5   7.00 - 8.00   Half 3.50 - 4.00   Splits 2.25

French Champagne: Bottle 10.50 up   Half 4.75 up

(Magnums and Jeroboams also available)

The BOURBON, GASLIGHT, NAPOLEON and BIENVILLE ROOMS
available for Breakfast and Luncheon Parties

Dejeuner a la Fourchette

Grilled Grapefruit with Kirsch .60   Baked Apple with Cream .40

Fresh Fruit Compote .60   Strawberries with Cream .60

Creole Cream Cheese .40   Sliced Georgia Peaches with Cream .40

Sliced Bananas with Cream .40

Stewed Prunes .35

Cantaloupe and Honeydew Melon Balls .40

EGGS HUSSARDE — 1.75
Marchand de Vin Sauce over grilled ham and tomato on toast. Poached eggs and Hollandaise sauce.

EGGS BENEDICT — 1.50
Broiled Ham and poached eggs on crisp toast. Hollandaise sauce.

EGGS A LA TURK — 1.75
Shirred eggs with chicken livers, fresh mushrooms and red wine.

EGGS SARDOU — 1.75
Artichoke bottoms, poached eggs, creamed spinach and Hollandaise sauce.

CHICKEN LIVER OMELETTE — 1.75

POMPANO CLAUDET — 2.40
Broiled pompano. Finely chopped onions, garlic, parsley and chives.

TROUT VIN BLANC — 1.75
Lake trout. White wine seafood sauce.

ESCARGOTS AU BEURRE — 2.00

CHICKEN LIVERS FINANCIERE — 2.00
Livers in a sauce of red wine, fresh mushrooms and olives.

EGGS ST. DENIS — 1.50
Souffleed eggs and chopped ham served on croutons. Marchand de Vin sauce.

EGGS BOURGINONNE — 2.00
Omelette with escargots and vegetables. Red wine sauce.

EGGS AUX FINE HERBS — 1.00
Omelette with finely chopped onions and parsley.

EGGS AUX CHAMPIGNONS — 1.00
Omelette with fresh mushrooms.

OMELETTE PARMESAN — 1.00
Omelette with Parmesan cheese.

CALVES LIVER — 2.00
Saute with bacon and hominy grits.

GRILLED HAM STEAK — 1.50
With eggs.

BREAKFAST CUT SIRLOIN — 3.00
Bearnaise.

LAMB CHOPS MIRABEAU — 4.50
Delectable combination of lamb chops, bacon, Bearnaise sauce and tomato sauce.

Hominy Grits .35   Brabant Potatoes .35   Hashed Brown Potatoes .35

Sauteed Bananas .50

SALADS: Waldorf .60   Blackstone .60

OMELETTE AUX RUM — 1.50
Jelly folded into an omelette. Sprinkled with confectioners' sugar and flamed with rum at your table.

OMELETTE WITH STRAWBERRIES — 2.00
Delicious Louisiana strawberries rolled into an omelette and flamed with brandy at your table.

PEACHES FLAMBE — 1.50
Peaches cooked in sugar and flavored with orange and lemon rind. Flamed with brandy at your table.

BANANAS FLAMBE — 1.50
Bananas cooked at your table in butter, cinnamon, brown sugar and rum.

CREPES SUZETTE — 1.75
The reigning queen of desserts made and flamed at your table.

CAFE BRULOT — 1.00
Coffee and chicory blended with cinnamon and cloves, orange and lemon rinds, cognac and orange curacao.

PETIT ORANGE BRULOT — 1.25
A quaint cup made from an orange holds the cognac. Flamed. Wonderful bouquet.

Cafe au lait .15

we were scraping up the last morsel and downing the tiniest remaining drop, I made an announcement.

"While you were out this morning," I told them, "and I was
writing letters, I had a telephone call from the wife of a Monsieur
Joseph who owns a restaurant on Bourbon Street. Madame Joseph
said she and her husband had heard we were here and were going
to see Cajuns and Cajun country. Monsieur Joseph, she said, is a
Cajun. She also told me *she* comes from Chicago. But Monsieur
Joseph wants to give us tonight one of his best dinners and tell us
some Cajun stories. We're to be there at eight o'clock, and
Monsieur J. sent word please to arrive with fine, big appetite."

Sophy regarded me dourly from across the table. "You ought
to learn something about a thing called 'timing.' This is *not* the
moment to talk about dinner. I guess the only thing for us to do
is walk all afternoon."

We did. But not until Miss Brennan had taken us across the
street and into the Old Absinthe House that the Brennans now
own and run. Kat told in detail how I had tried to find it the first
night. I sometimes wish my dear friend did not feel a need to be
quite so informative. Miss Brennan was tolerant of our urgent
plea not to be given anything to drink there, let alone absinthe,
and let us enjoy the place for itself, with its fine old smoky low-
beamed ceiling and dim light. She took us upstairs to see a hide-
away of Lafitte's, a separate story without windows, concealed
between the first and third floors. There, the legend goes, General Jackson and the pirate planned the Battle of New Orleans.
At the doorway to an inner dark room, Miss Brennan stepped
aside and we were suddenly confronted by a reproduction of the
actual scene done with wax figures, life size, and startlingly
realistic at first glance.

As we stood in the doorway of that musty, windowless room,
Miss Brennan told us another story, of Andrew Jackson and a
judge. When Jackson was preparing the city for defense, prior
to the Battle of New Orleans, a judge endeavored to thwart what
he termed Jackson's high-handed procedure. Whereupon Jackson had raised his hand a little higher, and put the entire city

under martial law. After the battle he had courteously returned it to civil law. The judge had immediately convened court and fined Jackson one thousand dollars for contempt of court. Popular opinion had endorsed the judge's decision, but popular subscription by the entire citizenry of New Orleans had paid the fine.

I might have learned the name of the judge and verified the story by looking it up in a source book. But I'd rather keep it in my memory as it was told—in a dark room on a sunny day, where a pirate and a general once worked together, in a French tavern that is still a French bar, owned by an Irish family.

We returned to our hotel, shed our furs, picked up our guidebooks and set out again. We explored Dauphine Street, stopping frequently to point out an exquisite balcony railing or a lovely doorway; but we stood a long time in front of Number 505. This was the "little house in Dauphine Street" where the Audubon family lived and nearly starved, while in 1821 and 1822 the artist was working on a series he was to call *Birds of America*.

The rest of the afternoon we walked. How we walked! Across St. Louis Street, peeking in between the bars of tall iron gates to see the lovely courtyard of what is now the Christian Women's Exchange. There a card reads, "Stuffed toys, Dolls and Preserves may be purchased. Orders taken for baby clothes. Antique furniture, Silver, China and Glassware are on sale." And as though this were not wide enough variety, there are also, "Pleasant rooms for women at moderate prices."

I was the first to give up. I told the four stalwarts if we continued walking I would have to take off my shoes. This threat brought them to a halt, and we hailed taxis; several, because we were scattering to pay calls on friends and acquaintances on our separate lists. But I was allotted the first cab by asking if anyone minded my sitting down on the curb while I waited.

We met later for tea at a beautiful old house that belongs now to the Lawrence Williamses. It is not far from the Sterns' house but while the Sterns' house has deliberately followed the tradition of a Southern mansion because of love for that pattern, the Williamses' house is the tradition itself. There is, of course, a lower entrance flush with the ground, but for the gentry an entrance reached by a flight of steps and a walk around a long gallery to the wide front doors. The interior fulfilled our happiest anticipation and so did the Williamses, whom we had not met. They were charming, hospitable and undismayed by five women, all of us unknown to them.

Back at the hotel we found a message from Monsieur and Madame Joseph, telling us not to come to their restaurant until nine o'clock when there would be fewer other diners than we would find earlier, and Monsieur Joseph would thereby be able to give us greater attention. It was welcome news. Ellen and Kat celebrated it by going to their rooms immediately to take a nap.

We were rested when we left at nine for the restaurant. My legs had stopped aching, I was happy in my shoes, and, we admitted to one another shamefacedly, we were all of us ravenously hungry.

Joseph, Madame Joseph, Madame Joseph's daughter and a waiter took us to a table in a room to ourselves, all talking at once, and so were we. Joseph is tall, slender, pink-cheeked. His hair is sparse, his vitality is not. Madame Joseph is small, dark-haired, recently married to Joseph, having met him on a sight-seeing trip to New Orleans from her native Chicago. She is still bewildered by such an outcome of a vacation trip, but delighted with it. Her daughter by a previous marriage is a student at Tulane, about to be married and go with her husband to Philadelphia, where they will continue work toward their doctorates. I doubt that Joseph knows what a doctorate is, but he and his step-daughter are thoroughly congenial and mutually appreciative. She left us shortly. She had to study, she explained.

Joseph nodded his head in admiration. "Books and books she reads. *Mais*, she learns from me to cook, too. Can you believe that thing?"

Joseph obviously found such a combination almost impossible to believe. His English is unconventional to benighted Northern folk, and it has a splendid flourish. Joseph does not say, "I like." He says, slapping his chest resoundingly, *"Me, I like."* And Joseph likes many things. He enumerated some of them after he had poured us each a glass of wine and drunk our health. "Me, I like *first* fun," he said, "all Cajun, they like fun."

"*That's* the truth," Madame Joseph murmured. She was sitting beside him.

Joseph gave her a hearty buss on the cheek, a smack on her rear, and continued. "Then, me, I—all Cajuns—like good food, very good food. Lots good food. And then good drink. Lots good drink. But not for getting drunk. I, me, not like getting drunk— is not fun." He lifted his glass to us. "Then me, I, like, Cajun like, women."

"They seem pretty far down on the list," Ellen observed thoughtfully.

"Is end of list," Joseph agreed happily, "but is maybe best. All fun. Me, I like all fun."

Kat, I think, felt the conversation was getting a little out of hand. "What are we going to eat?" she asked decisively.

Joseph kissed his fingers and rose from the table. "Me, I cook now."

I asked in some surprise if he was the cook as well as the owner of the restaurant.

"Me, I, am *all,*" was Joseph's answer. And he slapped his chest again. "Now," he continued, "we going to have oysters Bienville for some, and special canapé Joseph for others. Which you like?" he began with me.

I asked apologetically if I could have the oysters without any garlic. Garlic, I told him, or onion, makes me very ill.

"Could not be," Joseph assured me emphatically. He shrugged his shoulders. "*Mais,* if you think so, *bien*—no garlic."

He learned from the others their choice and left, promising to return soon. He put for us, in his place, he explained, a bottle of wine.

When he had gone we asked Madame Joseph the story of the house. She echoed our admiration of its beautiful proportions and detail. "I never get used to it," she explained. "It's so different from what I've been used to in the Middle West."

I told her that was my origin too and we nodded to each other in mutual understanding of the difference.

"There isn't a nail in the house," she began. "It was built entirely with pegs. Its date is 1835 and it belonged to Judah P. Benjamin. This is the Judah P. Benjamin house. You've probably heard of it."

Kat gave a startled exclamation and stared frankly openmouthed at Madame Joseph. "Why, for heaven's sake," Kat said, and was almost stammering, "this is the house I've been looking for. I just can't believe it. Judah P. Benjamin," she was finally able to explain, "was the law partner of my husband's grandfather. They went through Yale together and later set up a law practice here. One of the last things my husband said was to be sure to see the Judah P. Benjamin house. But I certainly didn't dream I'd be eating dinner in it."

Madame Joseph asked if we would like to see the rooms upstairs and we followed her up a broad stairway to rooms above, lovely in proportion, but empty now. If the restaurant prospers, Madame Joseph said wistfully, they hope to restore them in furniture to their original period and make them available for private, large dinner parties.

"It would be better to wait until after dinner," she said, "to visit the kitchen," though she wanted very much to show it to us. But Joseph would not take kindly any interruption while he was creating.

We returned to our table and almost immediately the waiter brought us the first course, oysters Bienville and the canapés. We tasted, we gave little moans of contentment, and after that we ate and scarcely a word was spoken. I have not eaten elsewhere oysters such as those, nor tasted canapés. I do not need to for comparison. I know where they are to be found with flavors so delicate and so subtly blended it would be impossible to separate and identify the ingredients. One thing I do know definitely. I will go back to Monsieur Joseph's restaurant.

Monsieur Joseph came in with the next course and, like any artist who has just completed a creation, looked both pleased and anxious. The pleasure deepened when we assured him separately and in chorus we had never tasted anything more to our liking than what we had just finished. The next course was fish—redfish, we learned—with a sauce that was generically hollandaise but made so sophisticated by additions to its basic ingredients it was difficult to realize its origin was in a simple double boiler.

Monsieur Joseph shook a finger at it reprovingly like a parent admonishing a recalcitrant child. "You are bad with me tonight," he said. He turned to us. "I do not know what gets into it. Everything is like always to start with, but he gets bad. Twice I am so mad I throw him out. This is the third."

I told Joseph I didn't know what had got into it either, and I was sure he wouldn't tell me but "he" was certainly not bad this time. "He" was wonderful.

With this rich dish we had a crisp, green salad and that was all, except for a bottle of Graves 1944, delicate, and pronounced by our sommelier, Sophy, "out of this world." It was a perfect meal. We weren't surfeited by extraneous oddments. We were given the specialités and allowed to savor them without confusion.

Kat accepted a dessert, an ice, mint-flavored. In the nick of time I forestalled her customary explanation for indulging in a sweet: "I like to get the taste of the other food out of my mouth." Under the table I kicked her smartly on the shin.

When coffee was offered Darn looked at me inquiringly. "Okay?" she asked, and then turned to our hosts. "Miss Kimbrough," she explained, "wouldn't let us have coffee in a restaurant our first night here."

Had she not been on the other side of the table from me, I would have kicked her, too.

Ellen has always a tendency to explain things. "Miss Kimbrough had other plans for us," she told the Josephs, "but they didn't exactly work out. She tried to take us—"

I interrupted loudly. "We came to hear about Cajuns. Never mind about our little episodes. Tell us about your part of the country, Joseph. Where do you come from?"

"St. Martinville," Joseph answered, "that is St. Martin Parish."

We had learned that in Louisiana counties are called parishes. So we were not misled into thinking of Joseph as a religious man identifying himself with his church.

"You must go there and you must eat coush-coush."

Madame Joseph interrupted. "That's right. You try it, they're all crazy about it. I don't care much for it myself."

Kat wanted to know what on earth it was.

"It's cornmeal," Joseph told her, "browned in pork fat. Is beautiful."

Kat shuddered slightly, but made no comment.

"We don't get back much any more," Madame Joseph spoke again. "We're too busy here. And Joe's learning to play bridge. He's crazy about it. You ought to see the way he plays." She shuddered a little, too.

Joseph grinned and banged his fist on the table. "By Gar," he shouted. "I love that game. Is cultured, too. I get culture from the bridge. I love the double. Is fun."

"Don't they play bridge in St. Martinville?" Darn asked.

Both the Josephs laughed at such an idea.

"In St. Martinville?" Joseph repeated. "*Jamais!* You know what they do in St. Martinville? They go to bed with the chickens. And have lots of babies. People there have big, big families. No bridge."

Kat broke in abruptly and decisively. "We'd better be going home," she said.

Joseph was dismayed. Why for? he wanted to know, must we go so early? We should be like his Mama. When he and Madame Joseph finished work and closed up the restaurant it was generally about three in the morning. Then they would go home and his Mama would be waiting. They all lived close together. "We are a family." He would mix up cognac eggnogs for his Mama, his wife and him. Mama was eighty-eight. She would not like to go to bed without a cognac eggnog first.

We regretted we did not have Mama's stamina, we told Joseph, and therefore must go home. We shook hands all around. The

Josephs went to the door with us, and as we left them, Joseph said earnestly, "Me, I wish for you to have fun to live, like Cajun."

It was a happy wish, we told him, and we thanked him for it.

Chapter Six

On Monday afternoon at three o'clock we were in a station wagon leaving New Orleans and heading west for Napoleonville, seventy miles away. Our objective had been determined by way of *The Saturday Review*. A month before when we had been vaguely talking about the trip, Sophy had come upon an advertisement in that publication and had read it to me.

"Open All Year," it had said, "Mr. and Mrs. Edward Munson, Glenwood Plantation House, an historic ancestral home located in romantic Acadian country." The address was Napoleonville, Louisiana.

It was the first clipping that went into a folder I had marked "Louisiana Trip?" with a large question mark. The folder was bulging now, but the first clipping was still out in front.

Getting away from New Orleans had not been all peaches and cream. It had involved such intricate planning as to make Kat feverish with pleasure and the rest of us well-nigh distracted. First of all we had had to hire a station wagon, the only vehicle that could accommodate, comfortably, all of us. Sophy, self-nominated but unanimously elected, had taken on this assignment. She had also proposed herself as the driver, with no changing about, and had carried that election, too.

We had selected Darn's as the room to keep while we were away, and moved there the bags and clothes we were not going to take on the trip. There had been considerable traffic in and out of that center, and more than considerable congestion, because, although Darn's was the largest closet, and that had been the reason for selecting her room, the number of hangers had not been increased in spite of frequent appeals to the housekeeper. Ellen had been the last depositor and fretted a little over the small space left to her. We'd apologized but had suggested she should have come earlier. She need not have told us the reason for her tardiness. We would have guessed it, but she told us anyway. It had been her breakfast egg. This time the egg had been too hard, "although," she'd protested, "I don't see how I could have explained what I wanted more carefully."

And Kat had echoed, "I don't see how you could. I heard you."

We had not brought so many clothes that they jammed the closet because we had wanted to present a dazzling appearance with frequent changes of costume. It was simply because we had been unable to learn from anyone what temperature to expect. We had had a good many conferences on the subject, and the result had been an overloading. Each of us had brought a heavy suit, one of medium weight, and one light, and an old one for the motor trips that we wouldn't mind "sitting out." This cataloguing had caused Ellen a tremor of uncertainty. "All my suits are old," she had said, "and that makes it hard to decide which one to sit out."

We had followed the same principle of being prepared for anything with our dresses: wool, silk and cotton. Consequently, we were overweight in every way. Now we know that for Louisiana in November a medium-weight suit, such as flannel, a warm topcoat to wear over the suit if the evening is chilly and sometimes in the daytime, and silk dresses are all you need. The climate is not hot enough at that time of the year for cottons, nor would they be appropriate, because Louisiana is a working State, not a vacation playground like Florida.

The only part of our equipment we felt just right in number was our shoes. Each of us had brought three pairs of walking shoes for sightseeing, one dressier pair for possible cocktail parties or the like, and one pair of evening slippers. Each of us has tramped many a street in many a country, guidebook in hand,

and, pooling our experience, had agreed vehemently that a change of shoes at midday will keep you on your feet until evening.

After the stowing away in Darn's room had been accomplished, Sophy had gone out to visit each of the automobile renting agencies she had listed from the telephone book. Kat had gone to buy the crystal chandelier for Priscilla and the girandoles for herself, and Ellen had accompanied her. Darn had gone separately to buy, she was not sure what, or at least she wasn't telling and she wanted no one with her. I had gone drifting with my guidebook.

We had met again back at the hotel at half past two, everyone garrulous with success. But shortly after my arrival I had slid to the bottom of the popularity list, because I had reported my luncheon with a gentleman. It was not with whom I had lunched that had irked them, as each took pains to point out, but on what. We had agreed that socially it was everyone for herself and no elbowing in from any other member of the group. So when a friend of mine had written a man she knew and he had courteously asked me to lunch, my dear ones had thought it fine and had gone their separate ways. But when I'd come back and described buster crabs eaten at Antoine's, there had been what Sophy's father used to call, "Hell to pay up in Jones's Woods." I shouldn't have explained, I know it now, that a buster crab is small and succulent, neither hard-shell nor soft; it is without shell. It is obtained at the moment when the creature is changing its clothes. Then it is sautéed. With a crisp, green salad, dressed with a French dressing as made at Antoine's, and a glass of wine lunch becomes a dream, a poem. I'd said all these things. I should instead have told them, "I had a very nice lunch."

The others, I'd learned, had eaten sandwiches.

But Kat had found her chandelier and girandoles. Darn had bought what she wanted, but did not explain. And Sophy had brought back a station wagon. Sophy was at the head of the popularity list.

Our road out of New Orleans took us over the imposing Huey Long Bridge, and then we were on the highway. Darn at once began to read aloud from the WPA book, *The Louisiana State*

Guide. For a little while we doubted the accuracy of that excellent volume until we discovered that 411, which we were following, had New Orleans as its destination rather than its beginning. Therefore, for us, it must be read backward.

"Simple enough," Darn said, "except when computing mileage," and Sophy frequently requested this computation.

Inasmuch as any mathematical calculation to be made instantly casts about me an impenetrable fog, I find very little difference between going forward and backward. But when I said this Sophy answered that no one would dream of asking me to do anything mathematical anyway, and suggested I simply allow the rest of them to sympathize with Darn.

The day was warm and bright, so bright that we put on our dark glasses. That was one piece of equipment that had not turned out to be superfluous. The station wagon was bright, too, a shiny new Chevrolet. Sophy had got it from the U-Drive-It Car Company on Baronne Street, and it was to cost us $156.81 for two weeks. That, divided five ways, did not make extravagant transportation. Even with what we had left behind, we filled it, with bags, extra coats, cameras and five of us: two in the front seat, two in the middle and one on a single seat in the rear.

Our spirits rose high and so did our voices. "We're off to see the wizard, the wonderful wizard of Oz," we sang. Not one of our offspring was there to say, "Oh, mother." We could be as young as we felt.

Suddenly I broke off and pointed out the window to my right. "Girls," I said (we use this term to one another when our children are not around), "girls, look! That's the levee. We're riding along beside the levee of the Mississippi River. Lawk a'mercy," I added, "this is none of I."

Sophy said she would be surprised if it were not the levee since that would mean we were considerably off our track. Nevertheless, she was impressed, and without being asked drew the car to the side of the road and stopped. Darn left off reading the guidebook; we all climbed out of the car and up the bank that rose from the highway. It was a grassy bank, but the grass was brown

at this time of the year. The climb was fairly steep, but the top
flattened out as broad as a country road. Standing there we
looked down and across the wide, yellow Mississippi. We saw
a foolish little ferryboat come toward us and watched a capacity
load disembark at a landing—its capacity about twenty people and
two cars.

When we had seen the arrival successfully accomplished we
returned to our own car. Sophy pulled onto the highway again
and Darn resumed her reading of the guidebook. She read us
about the Plaquemine ferry that charges fifty cents for a five-
passenger car, operates on call from 6 A.M to 6 P.M. and is summoned by blowing your car horn. Kat's comment was that this
was both instructive and picturesque, but slightly irrelevant, since
what we had seen was not that ferry at all, and that Darn, for-
getting to reverse, was reading from the wrong end of 411. For a
little time after that Darn read us nothing at all. But happily, she
found her place in time to warn us that we were approaching the
Locke Breaux Live Oak, a sight that would be well worth our
slowing down to see. It would be difficult to pass by without noticing this magnificent landmark. It is a few miles beyond the little
village of Hahnville and is itself on the grounds of the Southern
Dairy Company, a property formerly owned by a Mr. Samuel
Locke Breaux of New Orleans.

The guidebook says it was his interest in the tree that first
brought it into prominence. I do not believe that proud ancient
needed the interest of Mr. Breaux. It dominates the surrounding
landscape by its own immensity and the beauty of its symmetry
and rich foliage. The lowest branches, curving down, sweep
the ground, and its top ones, so the guidebook says, are seventy-
five feet above. No wonder it is the president of the Live Oak
Society, and our reader told us from the guidebook about that
distinguished organization. It comprises over fifty members and
each of these is at least one hundred years old. To qualify for
membership, a candidate must measure at least seventeen feet in
girth four feet from the roots. Each member has a sponsor
who must furnish the history of his ward and furthermore guar-

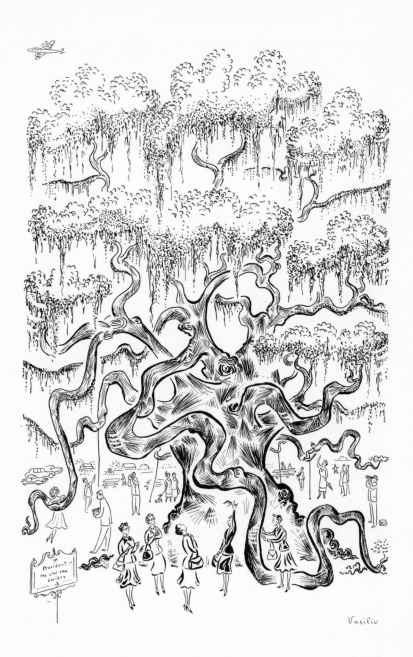

President —
THE LIVE OAK
SOCIETY

Vasiliv

antee its preservation. The annual dues are twenty-five acorns from each tree. These are planted in the Live Oak Nursery in Lafayette. One of the by-laws reads, "Members shall not be whitewashed. Violations of this law shall be punished by expulsion."

Our next stop was at Oak Alley, and though it is open to the public we were somewhat reluctantly admitted because we arrived just before five, which is closing time. We might have rung the doorbell earlier had we not stayed so long transfixed by the alley of live oaks that gives the plantation its name. This double row of glorious trees marches from the road that runs along the levee straight to the wide steps and the center columns of the beautiful house itself. This is not the entrance, however, but it is the first view one has, through a tall, iron fence, of the straight alley of astonishing trees and, at its far end, massive Doric columns. The house itself is in Greek Revival architecture, of plaster-covered brick, and not white as one might have expected, but a delicate pink. There are two galleries one above the other, and they do not run only across the front, but surround the house. These are details. The glory that is Oak Alley is the alley itself, twenty-eight oaks in double line, pointing up to twenty-eight Doric columns. The driveway a little beyond the alley proper leads circuitously to the door by which one actually enters.

On our way I exclaimed with delight over a charming *garçonnière* that we passed and Darn challenged me. "You've been talking about *garçonnière* and *pigeonnier*. I don't know the difference."

"Well," I explained, "one is for bachelors and the other is for pigeons, with or without families. In the old days when a son of the house was considered by his parents to warrant independence, I don't know whether he had to reach a specific age or not, he was given a little house some distance from the main residence. He could entertain his friends there and live in it, if he wished. It was a guest house for his use only. *Pigeonniers* were for the birds, because they and their house were considered such a decorative asset to a formal garden of the period."

This was the first piece of information I had been either able or allowed to give. But when I mentioned this Kat said she would appreciate it if, when I had anything further to contribute, I'd endeavor to follow the style of the guidebook: informative, without being long-winded.

The owner of Oak Alley was not at home, but a maid who was also a qualified guide by virtue of her wealth of information took us over the house. The rooms are beautiful but I would count it sufficient treasure to look again and again just at the Oak Alley and the pale pillars at its far end.

If I had not walked around to the front of the house for a last look down the alley toward the river, the remainder of the afternoon, and there was not much left, might have passed uneventfully. But leave Sophy for more than five minutes in a car alone with a map, and she will have found a short cut. The others had gone with me for a last look and Sophy had been left alone. We could not have been gone more than six minutes. But when we returned to the car, Sophy had a finger on the open map, a gleam in her eye, and I knew what both meant.

"Look here," she said, "just let me show you what I've found."

Kat, Ellen and Darn looked. They are obliging people. It would not have done anyone any good for me to look. In the first place I can't read a map, and in the second place no one can dissuade Sophy from a short cut. I heard her explain, as she pointed with her finger, that we had to retrace our steps a few miles anyway to Vacherie, because, while we were romantically looking at a view, she had learned from a man working in the Oak Alley grounds the road beyond was under repair and our best way to Napoleonville was back by way of Vacherie.

Having established that, without any room for argument, she continued. "Now look. La. Highway 20 is the route indicated all the way down to Thibodaux, then up again to Napoleonville. You can see for yourself it makes a V."

They agreed it did make a V.

"Well then," she went on, fairly shouting with excitement,

"I'm sure I can cut across and pick up Route 1 without going all the way down to Thibodaux."

Her little chorus of three nodded their respective heads and that was all she needed.

"All right," she said, "if *you* think that's the best thing to do," and that was a silly statement if ever I heard one, "let's get going."

Where we went I shall never know. I only pray not to pass that way again. The others said it was Ellen's and my fault we had to travel in pitch darkness because we were the ones who had insisted on stopping to see Evergreen Plantation, a neighbor to Oak Alley. We couldn't go inside because it is privately owned, but we had stood wistfully at its gates, charmed by this beautiful example, too, of Greek Revival. Like Oak Alley the house has Doric columns that rise from the ground to the roof and support wide galleries. Since the WPA guidebook was written, the place has been restored, and having read it was in disrepair and abandoned, Ellen and I were so delighted with the surprise of its restoration we had persuaded Sophy to stop to allow us to enjoy it. I had also been able to point out to Darn both a *garçonnière* and a *pigeonnier*, and she had traded for that bit of information an excerpt she had found in the guidebook, a charming detail proving the artistic fidelity of the designer. "Even the privies at Evergreen," the guidebook reads, "are built of brick and are Greek Revival in design."

It seemed to me we were no sooner on our way again than darkness put an end to further viewing. Either evening comes on more suddenly in that part of the country than in ours, or we had been so preoccupied with pillars, galleries and other beauties we had not been aware of its approach. This was no misty twilight; this was Stygian blackness through which we traveled. Once along the way I persuaded Sophy to stop. It was not easy. Her dislike of asking directions is in exact ratio to her rapture over a short cut. But I had seen ahead of us two men come out of a lighted cabin and stand talking on its doorstep. When we reached them Sophy did pull up, but I had to do the questioning. The interview was not reassuring.

"Can we reach Napoleonville by this road?" I asked.

I not only got back an answer in Cajun French but a difference of opinion between the two men. Cajun French is not easy to understand until one has become accustomed to it, and when it is spoken by two men talking against each other simultaneously, any listener can become addled, no matter what Sophy says about my inability to absorb directions. Furthermore, Sophy's technique of getting directions provides more obstacles than assistance. The instant a potential informer opens his mouth to answer the question that has been put to him, Sophy puts the car in gear and begins to move off. When the information is actually given, we are almost out of earshot and I am hanging out the window endeavoring to catch the words of the bewildered individual who is forced to shout. This has been the procedure on every motor trip I have taken with Sophy, and they have been many. It is what happened that dark evening in God-knows-where, Louisiana.

Sophy has since maintained I was the only one of the group to display irritability. The others, she says, were serene because they had confidence in her. My answer has been, and remains, that they have not taken as many short cuts with her as I have been led into. My contention is, furthermore, that I did not display irritability. On the contrary, I scarcely spoke at all. I may have murmured once in a while, "You and your short cuts." And I do remember that at one time I insisted we were not on a road at all because I had a definite sensation of riding over stubble and that probably we were going right through a sugar-cane field. Although Sophy insists this was not so, I still see no reason why it might not have been.

In the distance we could see a red glow that lighted up black chimneys beneath it. Since we had been told we were to go through sugar-cane country and that this was the grinding season when the mills grind night and day, what we could see was obviously a sugar mill in operation grinding sugar cane from the surrounding country, including a supply recently taken, I asserted, from the ground we were traveling over. We passed tremendous horse-drawn carts piled high with cane. The carts themselves were like outsized, loose-woven wicker hoppers such as one sees in France. These loomed up in the darkness unexpectedly. Once we passed perhaps ten or twelve of them moving slowly in close line.

It was not more than ten minutes after Sophy had maneuvered around this procession that suddenly we were on a highway, a highway that at that very point of intersection displayed a large sign bearing the route number 1, the very highway Sophy had said we would find. She was, I felt, and said, offensively smug about what I considered entirely a chance meeting. The others, who had been dozing, roused and congratulated her with repeated cries of admiration and praise.

In another fifteen minutes we saw ahead of us another sign, this time not the designation of a route but the identification of Glenwood Plantation House, a few yards ahead and on our left. We turned in the driveway and as we moved toward the house proper we could see, even in the darkness, the outline of trees over wide lawns—outlines of such size they could only be live oaks. We stopped at a doorway under a porte-cochere and, at the sound of our wheels on the gravel drive, the door opened, two large dogs rushed out immediately followed by a tall, slender man with a toy fox terrier at his heels, and a very diminutive lady at his side. Light came from the house through the open door behind them and we could see as they moved toward us that both were smiling a welcome, and instantly they began to talk simultaneously. "Come in, come in," they said, "we're so glad to have you at Glenwood. Don't bother with any of those bags. We'll have them taken up. You must be so tired."

We were shaking hands all around within a minute, and being propelled up steps, across a porch and into a wide hall that was warm and lighted, and welcoming. These were our hosts, Mr. and Mrs. Munson, and we introduced ourselves individually to them.

They led us up a stairway to a broad hall on the floor above with open doors along either side of it. Mr. Munson was slow and easy, Mrs. Munson quick and anxious. Would we, she asked, like this room or, almost running ahead, would we prefer the next? We must take whatever we liked best, she did so want us to be comfortable.

Mr. Munson leaned against the side of a doorway. "As soon as you settle," he said, and grinned, "I'll have the bags brought up."

It wasn't easy to settle because each room into which we peeked had a particular charm, and each one to our surprise and pleasure had its own bath. All the beds were four posters and looked deliciously comfortable. Each room had a name on the door—"Cherokee Rose," "Azalea" and the like, and the whole furnishing gay and charming. Ellen and Kat finally took root in an end room with sloping ceiling, one bed in an alcove, the other in the room proper. Sophy and I lodged down the hall from them, and Darn across from us in "Cherokee Rose."

Mrs. Munson suggested we might come down to dinner as soon as we had freshened up, but Sophy asked if we might have a half hour's leeway because, she explained, "There are some things I want to take out of my shoebag."

We dined at a long table. The only other guest was Mrs. Farley, who was charming and, we learned, a teacher of mathematics in the local school. Hearing this, my friends seemed to find it relevant to tell her that as an undergraduate at Bryn Mawr I had established a record in mathematics, entering with a 26 in algebra, the lowest at that time ever recorded. After that piece of information Mrs. Farley was particularly gentle with me, as one is with persons of lower than average mentality.

The dinner itself could not be included on any diet but would be high on anyone's good eating list. This was more than good eating, this was eating to make one grow dreamy-eyed at the mere remembering of it. We began with a crabmeat ravigote, moved on to soup that was a rich gumbo, then broiled chicken, broccoli with hollandaise sauce, sweet potatoes, and for dessert pecan pie. I cannot say what gave the hollandaise the consistency of a soufflé, light yet firm, but I can share the recipe for the sweet potatoes because I coaxed it from Mrs. Munson. And here it is: Parboil sweet potatoes, not yams, and Mrs. Munson was emphatic about this, in the skin. Then peel and slice into a casserole; sprinkle with light brown sugar, pour over that a little orange juice, a little brandy to taste and finely chopped pecan nuts. Put into the oven until the sugar is well melted. I do not usually eat dessert; I have to munch Ry-Krisp and dry lettuce for too many days afterward. But I ate the Munson pecan pie and I voice the sentiment of all of us when I say, "Bring on the Ry-Krisp and lettuce, I'll not complain so long as I can have a piece of that pecan pie." It has to be eaten at Glenwood Plantation House, however; the recipe is old in the family and kept a secret among its members.

Mrs. Munson led the way to the drawing room where she said we would have coffee. As we followed her Mr. Munson explained the divisions of Louisiana according to coffee. This was very important for us to know, he said. "The last port of good coffee is Lafayette to the west, Bunkie to the north, and Mobile to the east. When you're beyond those boundaries," he insisted, "the coffee's terrible. You might as well be up North."

We had *café brûlot* at the Munsons', and this is not just coffee, it is a decoction and a ceremony. Mrs. Munson sat on a couch at the far end of the room from us as we seated ourselves near the door from the hall. In front of her was a low coffee table and on this a tray with a silver bowl in the center, smaller than a punch bowl, around it a ring of cups—very special cups, tall, slender, without a handle, white with a pink border and as decoration the figure of the devil in a coral shade, flowing cape and all. I remembered as I looked I had seen a duplicate bowl and cups in a window of an antique shop in New Orleans and had not known what they were for. Simultaneously I saw myself on a couch in my own living room in New York behind just such a set, and came back to the Munsons with something of a start at the sound of my own name.

"This is a recipe I can give you," Mrs. Munson was saying. And as she brewed she explained. "You must always make it in a *café brûlot* bowl, like this one. We use two lumps of sugar to each person, and then put in a few extra. The two lumps per person is because in these parts we say take one for yourself, and one for the industry." She poured and stirred as she talked.

Mr. Munson standing at the door said, "Ready?"

Mrs. Munson nodded.

Mr. Munson switched off the lights. Mrs. Farley, sitting at a table, turned out the lighted lamp on it. The room was in complete darkness. Mrs. Munson struck a match to the alcohol in the tray. The flame, bright blue, rose quickly, surrounding the bowl. Mrs. Munson took up a long silver ladle I had seen in the bowl. The end of the handle to which she put her hand was wood. She spooned into the bowl and lifted high into the air the ingredients placed there, but what we saw was a running sliver of flame, up from the tray, filling the ladle. Up and down, dipping and pouring, she carried the dancing, bright blue flame, and laughed with the pleasure of a child at our exclamations of astonishment. When the flame died out, and she had added the coffee, Mrs. Munson ladled it from the bowl into the *brûlot* cups. Though I seldom drink coffee and never at night, this was the night I drank *café brûlot*, ate pecan pie and slept like a child.

Here is the recipe for *café brulôt*.

    1 cup of brandy or cognac
    2 lumps of sugar per person
       (and 10 to 20 lumps over)
   30 whole cloves
   ½ orange peel—very thin
   ¼ lemon peel—very thin
    2 sticks whole cinnamon, broken in small pieces
    1 quart Louisiana dark-roast drip coffee

Put spices, peel, sugar into *brûlot* bowl.
Pour brandy or cognac over these.
Pour a little alcohol on tray *under* the bowl, and light it.
Stir contents in bowl until the heat from flame around it ignites the brandy in the bowl. Ladle up and down, letting it burn a few minutes before adding Louisiana coffee. Extinguish all lights in room when lighting alcohol. Turn on lights *after* coffee is added.

Before sleeping we went out again with Mr. Munson to see a sugar mill working at night. At six-thirty all I would have asked was dinner and permission immediately after to crawl into bed. But that dinner and the *café brûlot* had made new women of all of us and we were as eager to go as if we had spent the entire day indoors dawdling. As we drove the four or five miles to the mill, Mr. Munson told us something of the history of the sugar cane region; how once all the land had belonged to individual plantation owners, each plantation not less than a thousand acres, and how each owner had ground his own cane. But in 1927 bad floods had come that had ruined their crops, and before any had recovered, the Depression, like the flood, had engulfed them. That was the end of the big land holdings. Men like Mr. Munson, whose grandfather, coming from Massachusetts in 1820, had bought Glenwood Plantation, had had to sell their acres or had lost them to the bank. Now the individual holdings were small, but the co-operative mills were flourishing.

I asked why the mills operated at night and Mr. Munson explained that the grinding season is a short one, three months at best. It would close at Christmastime. The cane must be harvested and ground before the first freeze, not because of the freeze itself but the inevitable after-thaw that would rot the crop. Accordingly, for those three months the mills never stop.

Mr. Munson paused and laughed, "Everything else does though," he added. "Talk to any of the Cajuns and they'll tell you what they're going to do *'après la roulissant'*—go to the city, repair the house, get married. You don't find any marriages during the grinding."

Long before we reached the mill we could see a glow in the sky from the furnaces. I have seen that glow in South Chicago where the steel mills are and thought it nothing remarkable. But at Bayou Lafourche it was a remarkable and an incongruous sight. Here was an industrial plant in the center of fields of sugar cane in a flat countryside. No little town was disclosed by its glow, no sign of any commerce; not even streets with houses and people sleeping in them; only the narrow country road on which we traveled, vividly white against the monotone of the fields. These roads are topped with crushed shells.

In the last half mile along the road with us was a line of wagons such as we had seen on our short cut, each piled to overflowing with stalks of sugar cane.

"They're waiting to be weighed," Mr. Munson explained, as we eased past them. "Every man has his load weighed as it goes in. That's what determines his share of the profits."

At this distance, and we were almost at the end of our trip, we first caught the smell. But if there were no sight of, nor sound from the mill, the smell would indicate its whereabouts. We were aware of it simultaneously but not happily and we said so loudly.

Mr. Munson laughed at us. "If this had been a warmer night," he said, "with the car windows down, you'd have caught that a lot sooner. And I can tell you," he added thoughtfully, "in the bad years we'd have given anything for a wind to blow that smell to us around here. We'd rather have that in our noses than all the perfume from France."

The smell is not unbearable, but it's no French perfume. I grew up in Chicago, I know what a hot summer breeze from the west can bring from the stockyards. But this is more enveloping because it is heavier and sweet, too sweet, yet overlaid with a sourness of fermentation; but within five minutes or so of our first sensing it, we became accustomed and oblivious to it.

Mr. Munson parked the car in an enclosed yard that encircled the plant. The entrance to the building is at the top of a flight of stairs. Pausing there a minute to look back over the way we had come, I saw below me, on the side of the mill opposite the entrance we had used, a single railroad track, and on this, under a sort of porte-cochere, a freight car. A moment before I had felt far away from the things I knew, both in place and in time; in a place where the air was heavy with fermented sweetness, and the only people in an empty countryside driving wagons of another day, and even country, and speaking when we had hailed them a French that has not been spoken in France since the eighteenth century. And now I was looking down at a freight car loading the product that the roaring, bounding machinery on the other side of the doorway on which I stood was preparing.

"Lawk a mercy," I thought, and followed the others inside.

I cannot tell the process that we saw, being neither chemist nor engineer, but it was beautiful to watch. We walked along narrow galleries, went up and down stairs from one level to another, looked over a gallery rail down into a great cauldron where a coarse, thick sugar substance moved sluggishly around and around. Over the clamor of the machinery we shouted to workmen introduced by Mr. Munson, who knew them all, and were told by them about the constant testing for temperature changes, and the proper consistency in each stage of the dissolution from stalk to sugar. We saw cane syrup, heavy and dark, bubbling in a vat, and as we left we saw pouring into the freight car sugar that was granulated now, but still, even after the washing processes we had seen, carried something of the earth in its yellow clay color.

Mr. Munson reached into the chute that was carrying it and took enough to drop into my hand. It didn't sift from his hand to mine. It was a solid mass, sticky to feel, and it melted slowly on my tongue. I asked where it was being taken.

"Why, to a refinery," Mr. Munson told me.

"In a city, I suppose?"

"Oh certainly," he answered. "That's where the refineries are."

"Well, that's how it is, I guess," I said, and couldn't explain what I meant; seeing in my mind women with little fingers quirked, holding teacups and saying, "One lump, please," and feeling a silly pang that this strong, earthy substance must be refined.

When we turned into the driveway at Glenwood and were home again, Darn broke into our chorus of thanks for an unforgettable evening. "Is this the way we went?" she asked. "I thought it took us longer."

Mr. Munson stopped the car at the door. "No," he said, "this isn't the way we went. I thought I'd try a short cut."

Sophy was sitting beside him. She turned to face him, and grasped his hand. "Thank you very much, Mr. Munson," she said.

Chapter Seven

I WAS WAKENED EARLY NEXT MORNING BY THE SOUND OF a voice in the hall outside Sophy's and my room. It was a small voice not quite whispering, not quite speaking aloud, but it had sufficient volume to bring to me overtones of anxiety. I sat up in bed puzzled, and simultaneously Sophy in her bed raised her head, looked inquiringly at me and at the door. "What do you think is going on out there?" she asked.

I didn't know, I told her, but I had every intention of finding out. I got out of bed, went over to the door, listened a moment, then opened it and peeked out. At first sight I had no more idea than I'd had a moment before of what was going on, because what I saw was Mrs. Munson on her knees in front of Darn's door. Her back was toward me but her face was pressed to the keyhole and her arms were moving in a rapid, though small circle, first one way and then reversed. She seemed to be turning the doorknob. I could also make out that it was Mrs. Munson who was talking, and could hear what she was saying but it was not clarifying.

"Don't be excited, I beg of you. Dear Mrs. Erdman. It is Mrs. Erdman, isn't it? Oh yes, of course it is. I'm so distressed I couldn't for a minute remember how you had divided up last night. But don't be upset, there's no danger. The carpenter is coming."

I turned back into our room and hurried for my dressing gown and slippers.

Sophy from the bed repeated, "What on earth is it?"

I told her I hadn't the faintest idea. Darn seemed to be upset about something and wouldn't let Mrs. Munson in. I was on my way to find out the trouble. I joined Mrs. Munson at the door, touched her lightly on the shoulder.

She jumped to her feet, turned around, looked at me with an expression of concern, and clasped her hands together. But before she could speak I heard Darn's voice from the other side of the door.

"Now, Mrs. Munson, if you'll just let me talk a minute."

"Oh dear, oh dear," from Mrs. Munson.

Darn went on, her voice soothing and slow. "I'm not in the least upset, it's perfectly all right."

Mrs. Munson interrupted. "I'm glad you've come, Miss Kimbrough," she said. "Will you keep talking to her, just to reassure her we're doing everything possible while I go down and see if I can help Edward. Only I'm afraid the telephone's out of order." She hurried off.

I squatted on my haunches. "What is all this?" I asked, and I felt a little flustered myself. "Can't I come in?"

Darn's voice was serene. She even chuckled. "I wish you could," she answered. "I'd be happy to have you. But I'm locked in."

"Whoever on earth did such a thing?" I demanded.

"Don't be a fool," came back from the other side of the door. And this time the voice was a little testy. "I locked myself in."

"Well," I said, "this is where we started. We thought you'd locked the door and wouldn't let anybody in. So you've locked yourself in. It comes to the same thing. Now open up."

"I *can't* open up. I turned the key in the lock and I guess I was too vigorous. I broke it in half. The bottom half is still in the lock, so you can't unlock it from the outside because you can't get a key through."

"When did you find all this out?" I asked.

Mrs. Munson had come back up the stairs. She had obviously been running from the time she had left us. She was out of breath and a little moist. "I'm here, Mrs. Erdman," she said, gasping, "I'm here."

Darn answered *me* first. "It happened last night when I was ready for bed. The last thing I did was lock the door, as I always do in any hotel, or whatever. I certainly locked it all right."

Mrs. Munson's distress increased at this news. "Oh no," she said, "not since last night. You haven't been locked in all that time! I wouldn't have had this happen to one of our guests for anything in the world. Oh, why didn't you let us know—whatever did you do?"

Darn's voice resumed its placid tone. "I couldn't have called you," she explained, "unless I yelled and woke everybody up. And as for what I did, why, I climbed into bed and went to sleep. After all, I wasn't planning to go anywhere anyway. I did think of climbing down the trellis outside my window, but it looked more fragile than I am. Anyway, I'd only have been locked out of the house instead of in my room, and this is much more comfortable."

Sophy's voice broke into the conversation. "Well, when were you planning to spread the alarm? This is Sophy."

I looked over my shoulder. Sophy, in dressing gown and slippers, had brought a chair from inside our room, placed it in the open doorway and was sitting back in ease and comfort, enjoying the scene.

"Hi, Sophy," Darn called back, "glad to have you join the group. Sorry if I waked you."

"Think nothing of it," Sophy answered. "I haven't heard a sound from our heavenly twins up the hall. This evidently hasn't reached them. I was awake anyway. Had you planned to get in touch with us eventually?"

Mrs. Munson broke in. "Oh, I think I hear someone at the door. This may be help. I do hope so. Will you excuse me, please?" She left our group.

Darn called out, "Take your time, Mrs. Munson. Don't hurry, I'm fine," and then answered Sophy, "I thought when the rest of you went down to breakfast somebody might notice I wasn't there, and come upstairs to find out why. I'm not sure any of the rest of them would notice, but I did think you would, and that you'd be the one to come up after me."

I interrupted. "I think I'll go on back to my room and get dressed," I said, "so long as you think I wouldn't be interested anyway."

"Darling," Darn called after me quickly, "I didn't think for a minute you wouldn't be *interested*. I only thought you wouldn't *do* anything, you'd just probably sit at the table wondering what might be the matter, offering all kinds of suggestions, but Sophy would be the one to come on up and find out."

"Why don't you get dressed anyway?" Sophy suggested to me. "You're always the last one. Get a head start."

"I'm not slow," I corrected Sophy. "It's just that I have long hair."

She edged herself in her chair a little to one side and I went past her into the room and shut the door, but not all the way. I heard Darn explaining that a maid had come, rapped on Darn's door and said, "I brought you some before-breakfast coffee. Breakfast is waiting whenever you're ready." And Darn had told her the situation; the maid had gone for Mrs. Munson, and therefore no one else had been approached with before-breakfast coffee.

I heard Mrs. Munson returning, talking volubly about the lock that had been there for certainly a hundred years and never given any trouble before, and Darn assuring her it had all been her own fault. I heard Mr. Munson's voice repeating his pleasure at having ". . . got you, Bill. It was beyond me. What with the dang telephone out of order to boot, we were in a fix."

Sophy backed into the room hastily, chair and all. "They got hold of a man somewhere. I think she'll be out of there in no time, now." She went into our bathroom to take a shower.

When I came out for breakfast the door of "Cherokee Rose" was open. Downstairs they were all having breakfast and had almost finished but, as I explained again, that is because I have long hair and have to braid it.

A maid asked if I would have fresh fruit or preserved figs, bacon and eggs, grits, pancakes, toast, and would I like Northern light-roast or Southern dark-roast coffee?

"Could I have tea instead?" I asked faintly. "And whatever fruit you have, but that's all."

Mr. Munson at the head of the table roared his disapproval. "You can't do that in *this* house. Why you might drop down in a faint. I've got a lot of places I want to take you all this morning."

"Give in," Sophy said. "We did."

I gave in.

Mrs. Munson came from the kitchen while I was eating. She was not entirely recovered from her distress that a guest of theirs should have been so troubled. No protests of Darn's nor corroboration from Sophy and me would convince her Darn had not been disturbed nor vexed, because, Mrs. Munson said, "*I* would have been very vexed. I would not like to be shut in, whether I wanted to go out or not. At least I would insist on doing my own shutting." Mrs. Munson is a diminutive Rock of Gibraltar and, like that other stronghold, cannot be pushed.

Kat and Ellen, the heavenly twins, were only rueful at having missed the whole thing. Nevertheless, they gave the impression they preferred missing it to having been wakened.

Mr. Munson said he had a plan, if that was agreeable to the ladies. At the word "plan" Kat turned on him a smile of such dazzling approval the dear man blinked a few times and turned a little pink.

Mrs. Munson spoke for him. "You were saying last night," she told us, "you were anxious to see real Cajun country, and this is it. So we thought Edward would drive you to some back country around Little Grand Bayou. It's pretty and you could meet some of the people, too."

We were off within the half hour, Mr. Munson at the wheel, the little fox terrier beside him; Mr. Munson had asked especially if she might come, too. Mrs. Munson had sweetly but firmly resisted our pleas that she come also. "I have things to do," she'd said, and when we had persisted had added with a delicious twinkle in her eye and twist of her upper lip into a little gamin grimace, "and anyway it'd be more fun for Edward, because he can tell you anything he feels like without me saying, 'Why, Edward, are you sure that's so?' I'm just teasing," she added with a quick breath, "there's nobody knows this country better than he does."

He began to tell us about it and the people in it as he turned the car off the highway onto a shell road. "We're going over to Little Grand Bayou," he said, "back of the village Brûlée St. Vincent. Our plantation, you know, is on Bayou Lafourche. That's a big one; it goes 105 miles."

Ellen wanted to know if he had traveled much on it.

Mr. Munson laughed happily at this question. "Traveled much," he repeated. "Well, I'd certainly like a nickel for every time I've gone up and down that bayou. When I was a boy it was the highway for us. That was the way we went to New Orleans, and we went frequently. Always went to New Orleans on the steamboat. Of course we never knew how long it was going to take to get there, but you could count on its being at least a day and a night, because we'd stop at pretty nearly every plantation, loading and unloading. My father had a warehouse right out on the bank like most of the other sugar planters. It'd take a boat several hours to load the sugar and molasses from there. If the family was going along we'd all be up by at least six o'clock in the morning. I can remember dressing by a kerosene lamp and stopping all the time to listen for that boat's whistle. But even when we heard it we reckoned it'd be hours before we'd be on our way. We knew all the captains, of course, and the captain would always come up and pay his respects when the boat docked, or sometimes he'd send up a present. Once, I remember we were having dinner—we had it in the middle of the day of course, at half past one—I'll never forget that particular dinner because right in the middle of it two deckhands came in carrying a huge cooked redfish. They brought it to my father right at the table, with the compliments of the captain."

Mr. Munson broke off his story abruptly with a loud shout. "Hey!"

We had all been as spellbound as children listening to a fairy-tale, and the shout startled us.

"There's my friend Landry," Mr. Munson explained. "Now that's something for you to see."

He pointed ahead and we saw a gray truck drawn up on the side of the road on our right. Mr. Munson stopped the car alongside the truck, leaned across Sophy sitting beside him and called, "Hello, my friend there."

In those few words Mr. Munson's accent changed completely. He had told about his boyhood in the slow sliding of syllables that marks a Southerner's manner of speech. But for all Mr. Munson's saying, "Hello, my friend," he might just as well by his change of accent have been saying, *"Allo, mon vieux."*

Mr. Landry was evidently a Cajun. He climbed down from the driver's seat of his truck. We left our car. We shook hands all around in the middle of the road. Mr. Landry led the way to his truck, stopped at the door opposite the driver's seat, and said, *"Entrez, s'il vous plait."*

Mr. Landry carries his establishment with him. It is a "rolling store."

I was just behind him and at his invitation I went inside. The interior was filled from bottom to top with commodities of almost every sort. They were neatly stacked on shelves that ran the length of the truck. Dry goods, canned goods, baby foods, cosmetics, bolts of material, and more. Mr. Landry rolls through the countryside a grocery, drug and dry-goods store combined. We bought from it coffee, dark roasted and with chicory, some crackers and cookies, and found all of them delicious. I should like to write to Mr. Landry for more of his coffee, but I do not know where he stops to pick up his mail.

After this pleasant interlude and delightful conversation, we left him with a customer who had arrived by car, and presently we were at Little Grand Bayou. The vegetation and woods were thick on either side of the water, except for a clearing where little shacks stood, and there were not many of these. Water hyacinths covered the surface of the water in big floating patches. There were few blooms but the leaves were bright and shining green. Along the banks we saw the twisted knees of giant cypresses, and from the branches above, Spanish moss trailed and swung a little in a light breeze.

We left the car and walked along the bank saying *"Bonjour"* as we passed to a man who was painting his shack, built like a houseboat, and perhaps it was one. But that morning it was wedged so well into the side of the bank it looked to me to be permanently there. I think I would like to live a while in that little house with the bayou water underneath and the cypress trees around. It had a jaunty look, tilted a little into the bank, and it was freshly painted, white with green trimming. A plank wide enough to walk carefully on, from its front door to the road, spanned a little branch of the bayou. I would not have chosen for mine any of the other dwellings. There were not more than half a dozen of these all told. None was painted. They were all above ground on stilts and could not have contained more than two rooms, but since the door to each one was open we could see inside as we strolled along, and they were shining clean; not a rug on a floor, but the floors scrubbed until they were almost white.

A young woman came from inside and stood in her doorway. We stopped to talk to her. Two small children peeked at us from behind her skirts; a baby on hands and knees crawled rapidly toward us. But as he passed, the mother, laughing, stooped down, scooped him up and settled him on her hip, her elbow crooked around him. She was pretty, with dark eyes, brown hair, pink cheeks; slender but with the look of health about her. The children were attractive, too, and the little boy who finally came out from behind her skirts was handsome. The mother spoke a little English and explained partly in English, partly in French, that the little boy went to school but had hurt his hand. The child proudly held up a bandaged hand. She was keeping him home for a few days. And her husband was away, "pulling cane."

I asked if I might take their picture and she moved out with her little covey to stand on the front stoop. Behind her in the room she had quitted I could see an iron double bed. I hadn't seen one like it since I was a child. This one had a patchwork quilt for a spread turned back to show coarse, yellowish sheets, all the bedding immaculately clean.

When I had taken the picture we said good-by and the children waved to us as we moved off.

Mr. Munson explained that "pulling cane" meant the husband was driving a truck, perhaps one of those we had seen lined up the night before.

At the next shack an old lady leaned out the window watching our approach. She rested her arms on a shelf just outside the window sill. Mr. Munson told us this shelf is called a *tablette*, that it's found outside almost every Cajun house and has a definite purpose. A dishpan is placed on it and the dishes are washed there through the open window. When that operation is completed the dishpan is tilted and emptied onto the ground below, so that the tiniest food scrapings removed in the washing can be picked up by the chickens. "That is how thrifty the Cajuns are," said Mr. Munson.

He continued about these people of whom he is obviously very fond. "They're strong and very healthy. If you were to drink the water from that bayou you might not be the better for it. But they thrive on it and on the kind of lives they lead. They had a death in this community last month, an elderly man of 104, but his widow's going strong. She's 98."

I asked how they made a living.

"Fishing," he answered, "trapping and harvesting cane, in the season. And they do well, too, on the Spanish moss."

"Great heavens," I asked, startled, "is it good to eat?"

Mr. Munson shook his head at such ignorance. "Lord no," he said. "They pull it and dry it and then they sell it for stuffing. A good deal of upholstered furniture, not perhaps the most expensive kind, but the great bulk of it, includes Spanish moss in the stuffing."

We came to the end of the row of little shacks; it was not long. We turned back, walking slowly along the grass-fringed bank of the bayou. The sun was warm on our backs, there was not a sound except our own voices and once a shiver of wings as we saw a big blue heron rise up from the water's edge on the opposite bank.

"Lots of good fishing here, too," Mr. Munson said. "These people rent out boats and act as guides. Mostly for people from New Orleans, and around. Folks from the outside for the most part don't know about this country. But if they come as somebody's guest they surely do get a pleasant surprise."

I said I was having a pleasant surprise, too, even though I wasn't a fisherman; just enjoying this strange, beautiful distant country, that was still so close to home. And I added wistfully, "I'd like to 'get to be,' as we say in Indiana, on the inside and not somebody from the outside."

Driving back to Napoleonville we passed another rolling store. Mr. Munson pointed to it and chuckled. "See that insignia on the side, that's pretty cute."

It was difficult not to see the insignia, a lurid orange sun with blindingly orange rays emanating from it.

"That's Eugene Foret's. He's got quite a business, more than one rolling store. Each one carries that sign. It's a pun. There are four rays, count them, and his name's Foret—Four Ray—get it? They're great ones for jokes," he told us after we assured him we had got it and explained the point to Kat, who is sometimes a little backward about jokes due to her leaning toward the literal. "The first thing for a Cajun is fun, then good food, and then good drink, but in moderation, he doesn't get drunk—and then women." This was precisely the list Joseph in New Orleans had given us.

Kat reminded us of this and added reflectively, "I notice women are still at the bottom of the list."

Mr. Munson resumed. He liked talking about the Cajuns.

"They're provident, they're thrifty and wonderful housekeepers. They don't give a rap for show. You notice how dilapidated those shacks looked on the outside."

"But how spotless they were inside," Ellen put in.

Mr. Munson agreed. "And under that spotless mattress I'd be willing to bet there's a sockful of money. You never hear of a Cajun having to let go his house or his property. It may not look like much but it's his."

As he was talking Mr. Munson suddenly slowed the car down and pointed to a house on our right, a little cottage with a tin roof set beside a magnificent grove of live oaks. "Now there's an example for you. Just what I've been talking about. That's the Simineaux house. It's been in that one family since it was got by a Spanish grant. And that's a long, long time." He picked up speed again and went on. "But don't get the idea that it's all work for them. Not a bit of it. As I said, it's fun first. Saturday, for instance, they don't work, they're getting ready for the dance, for the *fais do do*. That's what they call them."

"Why," Sophy interrupted, "that's the old nursery song. '*Fais do do.*' Go to sleep."

Mr. Munson threw back his head, gave a roar of laughter and very nearly ran us off the road. Swerving back into the lane he said, "Well, it's no go-to-sleep nursery rhyme here, I can tell you. It's a dance that lasts all night. They have them once a week anyway, sometimes twice. Sunday night's a big night for them, too. They start early and they dance the night through. Old and young. They bring the babies and put them on the floor under the benches. There's a row of benches that goes all the way around the dance hall. Of course during the grinding they give up the dances because so many of the men are working all night. But even during that season they'll maybe have a few. A Cajun's not going to give up his fun, no matter how hard he's working."

A little farther along the road a woman came out on the porch of a house. Mr. Munson stopped at her gate. The house was set back from the road with lawn and lovely trees surrounding it. She came to the gate smiling, even laughing at sight of Mr.

Munson, who was evidently a friend. They called greetings to each other and Mr. Munson introduced us collectively as guests from way up North.

I have forgotten the lady's name but not a particular thing she said, nor the shrug that accompanied it. Mr. Munson had asked about her figs and turning to us explained she had the biggest and the most delicious figs of anybody thereabouts.

Her answer was in French. "Not this year," and then in English, "too much bird, not much figs."

We paid no more calls, and in a few moments after the last one we were back on the main highway. I think the others, except for Mr. Munson, were as startled as I to find how close this thoroughfare was, with cars speeding along it, to the far-off silent country we had visited. In a few minutes we would be at Glenwood, but during the interim Mr. Munson, as he drove, asked if we would permit him to teach us a few things we really ought to know. We assured him we'd be grateful.

"Well," he said and was obviously relieved. "You don't know how it pains us when you all come down here and talk about beautiful camellias. It isn't camellias as in 'meet,' it's camellias as in 'met.' And please don't say 'pecan.' It's pecahn."

"As in Otto?" I suggested, but Mr. Munson had never heard of Mr. Kahn and I urged him to skip my remark and teach us more.

"Grits, then. Mrs. Erdman, at breakfast this morning you said to Miss Kimbrough, 'The grits are delicious.' They ought to be singular. We say, 'Grits is.'"

Darn assured him she would say it, too, from now on.

"Anything else we say wrong?" Sophy inquired.

"You're sure you don't mind my telling you?" Mr. Munson repeated.

His inherent courtesy and his discomfort at our blunders were having a hard time with each other, but we urged him to tell more.

"All right. Here goes. I know it's spelled 'crayfish,'" he said patiently, "but we call it 'crawfish.' I can't tell you why, but that's how it is."

"I've written all this down," Darn said as we got out of the car at Glenwood, "and we'll practice."

"I do *thank* you, ladies," was Mr. Munson's fervent answer.

Mrs. Munson came on the little porch to welcome us back and asked us where we'd gone.

"To Brûlée," I told her.

Mr. Munson, who had at that instant climbed out of the car, sank back in his seat again, clapped his hand to his head and shook it woefully. "No, no," he said, "excuse me once more, but every settlement is called a *brûlée*; that means a clearing. The one we went to was Brûlée St. Vincent. And by the way, folk in the *brûlées* call the grinding '*la roulissant*.' And as I told you last night, at this time of year, when they talk about getting married, having a *fais do do*, whatever, it's '*après la roulissant*.' One other thing; a settlement is called a *brûlée*, as I said, but also in Louisiana we don't talk about counties; they're called parishes here."

That we knew and told him so in chorus, glad to emerge even temporarily from dark ignorance.

We had no further instructions, not I'm sure because there were no other blunders to correct, but solely because we had no more time. We had to be on our way again back to New Orleans. We loaded the car, said our good-bys to the Munsons together with our promises to come back one day, and by half past twelve we were at Donaldsonville, waiting for the ferry to cross the Mississippi.

While we waited at the landing Kat climbed the levee behind it to the village and returned with bottles of Coke. We stood on the bank in the sun drinking it and looking out across the river at our little boat just leaving the opposite shore. And we talked again of how far away we had been with the big city New Orleans so close to us.

Sophy, the banker, reported that this happy interlude had cost thirty-seven dollars for the five of us, occupying three large rooms, each with a bath, and including the magnificent dinner and overwhelming breakfast.

The ferry docked; Sophy drove us on board, and paid sixty-six cents fare for the car and the five of us. We had taken the boat so as to return to the city along the bank opposite the one we had traveled on our way to Napoleonville, and immediately we were off the ferry we turned sharp right and were on the famous River Road that runs beside the levée. We paused at Hermitage Plantation House, driving in through the gates and up and around what was once a handsome dwelling, but is now in ruins. We saw its beautiful reflection pool, a characteristic feature of the landscaping of many of the plantations, a pool of such size and so placed as to reflect the whole of the house. A path through the trees leads to it, and there are stone benches around its border for restful enjoyment of the still beauty shimmering in the pond.

We paused at Bocage to look in wistfully, because it is not open to the public. We read from the guidebook it was built in 1801 by Christophe Colomb, a refugee from the French Revolution.

The Houmas House near the little village of Burnside is not open to the public but thanks to the intercession of Mr. and Mrs. Munson we were allowed to visit it. Its owner has donated years to a patient and meticulous work of restoration, and so we saw it very much structurally as it had been in the great days. The house itself is of two sections, the back very old with low ceilings, the front in the later period of lofty ceilings and large rooms, with one of the most beautiful spiral staircases I have seen. In the garden there is a gay little *pigeonnier,* and the house itself is flanked by a *garçonnière* on either side. I pointed these out to Darn. She told me crisply I need not bother any further, she was well able by now to recognize these features by herself. This house has Doric columns across the front. They rise two stories and cover three sides of the house.

We could not go in to Ormond. It, too, is not open to the public, but its splendor is clearly visible from the road.

In spite of our frequent and long pauses including lunch at a roadside restaurant, we were back at our hotel in New Orleans

and in our original rooms restored to us, in good time to unpack, settle in and even rest, before dinner.

We dined at Commander's Restaurant out near the Garden District and very popular there. Picking up my menu, and with a knowing smile at my friends, I began my order. "I'll have crawfish bisque," I said to the waitress.

And she answered, "You mean crayfish?"

Out of the whole of New Orleans my first oral exposure of my new knowledge was to a waitress who came from Brooklyn.

Chapter Eight

EVERY DAY BEGAN WITH A MORNING CRISIS. THE DEPENDABLE one was Ellen's breakfast egg, the unexpected had been Darn's lock-in. The morning after our return to New Orleans, in addition to Ellen's egg, the crisis was the loss of a pair of Kat's shoes. She reported the loss to the desk clerk over the telephone in Darn's room, because, she explained, Ellen was busy on their telephone about her breakfast egg.

Sophy, Darn and I were eating together, back to the old routine, in Darn's room and we were astonished by Kat's news. "Why on earth," I asked, "would anybody come into your room and take just a pair of shoes?"

"No one came into my room," was Kat's answer. "The shoes were outside my door."

This surprised us almost as much as the original announcement.

"What on earth were they doing outside your door?" Sophy wanted to know.

"They weren't doing anything." Kat seemed a little testy. "I put them there last night to be polished."

I shook my head in wonderment. "Well," I said, "I think our trip to the Cajuns has unsettled you a little. You've been carried away too far. This is still the United States, you know, where you can get ice water in your room, but you certainly do not get shoes polished outside your door. That's Europe, dear. Remember?"

"Is there any reason why they shouldn't be polished here?"

This is the kind of rhetorical question Kat particularly likes to fling down like a gauntlet in the hope it will be picked up, and a lively argument follow. We left it where she had dropped it, however. No one wanted a discussion. We had not had our coffee. We urged her instead to go back to her room and get her breakfast. We were sure her shoes would turn up.

They did turn up in the linen room, where, oddly enough, the Lost and Found desk is located. But we were never able to determine by what process of thought the chambermaid who had picked them up had reasoned that a pair of shoes placed in front of a door were lost articles dropped unknowingly by their owner.

The maid who had found them returned them and handing them over to Kat regarded her with some misgiving. "I never met anybody before," she said, "what kept their shoes *outside* the door. So when I see them I say to myself, 'Nobody mean those shoes to be there' and I took them to the Lost *and* Found."

Kat rewarded her but was all for giving, along with the recompense, a brief talk on European customs. Ellen placed a hand soothingly on Kat's arm and promised the maid, "My friend won't do it again."

I think, from the expression on her face, the maid went away with the impression that, in this instance, Kat had slipped her guards, but from now on would be more carefully watched.

We had returned from Napoleonville because of our engagement to lunch on *The Good Neighbor,* the boat belonging to the Port Authority, but generally referred to as the Mayor's Yacht, because during his term of office he is its host.

Mrs. Aldigé called for us about noon. She had telephoned us earlier she would be happy to drive us down to the dock and I had demurred. I didn't want to put her to so much trouble, I had said; there were five of us, we would crowd her, and we had our own car now, a station wagon. Let us, I urged, meet her at the dock or wherever she stipulated. But she would not hear of such an arrangement as I suggested. Her husband, she said, would be "real cross" at her if she allowed us to go to the party unaccompanied.

I gave in and the time was set for her arrival. When I hung up the telephone I repeated her message to the members of my happy band who were sitting on Sophy's and my beds listening and waiting for "the plans" to be revealed.

"It took you an awfully long time," was Kat's comment. "Why didn't you just ask what time she was coming and let it go at that? You aren't usually so excessively polite. I think you overdid it."

I had a reason and I told it. "I wasn't being polite," I explained. "At least that wasn't my motive. I wanted to go in our own car with Sophy to drive it. I'm silly about being driven. My nervous system's been shattered by lady chairmen who have driven me when I've been on lecture tours. Bless their hospitable hearts, they're so eager to show me the sights of their city, they never by any chance look at the road ahead of them. I have yet to sit beside a driver who doesn't turn to me, tell me the points of interest, and with one hand on the wheel point to them with the other. She sees everything except the light ahead that's turned to red, a car that has come out from a side street, or whatever. The only thing that's worse is for me to sit in the back seat. Then she turns all the way around. Someday I'm going to volunteer to straddle the hood of the car. At least then when she talks to me she'll have to look ahead."

Darn broke in. "Honestly, Emily," she said, "you and your imagination. How *can* you exaggerate like that?"

An hour or so later we climbed into Mrs. Aldigé's car at the entrance to our hotel. I sat in the back. Not ten feet beyond the entrance Mrs. Aldigé pointed out a building, and turning all the way around said, "I think you'd be particularly interested in that, Miss Kimbrough."

Ellen and Kat sitting in front with Mrs. Aldigé cried out simultaneously, "Look out."

Darn and Sophy on either side of me said nothing, but each gave a convulsive pinch on my thigh that left a mark. I was the only one comparatively serene. This was exactly what I had anticipated. But to my acute satisfaction my friends squirmed, gasped, pinched, turned to me faces drained of color and mouthed, "We'll be killed," or "Tell her 'never mind the sights.'"

I had thought at our first meeting Mrs. Aldigé was a thoroughly delightful woman. I think of her now with such a glow of affection as to make me want always from now on to send her a Christmas card each year to keep her vivid in my memory book.

I heard not one word more about my "exaggerating." Actually, when we left the car my friends could scarcely stand, let alone speak. I have no qualms about Mrs. Aldigé's own or her children's safety. I know she is at most times an able, a competent chauffeur. But I also know what happens to an able, competent driver when she is being hospitable to a stranger in her city.

The Good Neighbor is by no means the only way to see the river. Scheduled boats go every day and most of them more than once a day, across the river, down to the mouth of the Mississippi, to Grand Isle. There are almost innumerable excursions available. I am only sorry that time limited us to only one. But it was truly fascinating.

A yacht is not for me a customary method of transportation. At any time it would seem to me both a novel and de luxe conveyance. But after the days we had trudged the streets of New Orleans, guidebooks in our hands and perspiration on our foreheads, *The Good Neighbor* was for me as dreamlike as Cleopatra's barge. In the first place we didn't walk a step; we sat comfortably in the stern where a delectable lunch was served us. Furthermore, no one had to read from the guidebook; there were people around us who pointed out and explained every passing sight. Mrs. Morrison, the wife of the Mayor, was our hostess, and among the guests some we by now counted friends: Miss Brennan, at whose restaurant we had brunched on Sunday, and Mr. Tallant, whom we had met at the Grahams' party.

The sights themselves did not require pointing to catch our attention. They are dramatic: ships from every part of the world coming up the river or on their way down to its mouth and out to sea; and along the docks ships loading and unloading, drawn up in close single file in beautiful parade formation, bearing the names and the flags of Japan, Norway, Holland, Sweden, Liberia and many more.

What was pointed out to us was the reason for this dramatic formation. The river is so deep boats can stand alongside the docks without piers, and one of the advantages, and I don't suppose it was done purely for the effective picture it makes, is that when a ship is loading and there is perhaps a delay for cargo, or possibly another ship is coming in, the one already berthed simply moves up in the line and later backs to its place again, without any unwieldy maneuvering in and out.

The unloading of bananas was a sight to see. Lifted high in the air on a sort of conveyor belt they looked as though they were riding on a giant ferris wheel. I had never before seen more bananas at one time than hang in a grocery store. The ratio of that to the amount I saw swaying high in the bright sunlight above the Mississippi that morning was approximately as an acorn to an oak tree.

I said this to Mr. Baldwin, one of the guests in the party, and he nodded his head. "Well," he said, "you're not so far off. Those belt conveyors carry two thousand bunches of bananas an hour. That's an awful lot of bananas.

I asked where the conveyors took them, into a storage plant of some sort, I supposed.

Mr. Baldwin said no, they were loaded direct onto freight cars. "They start those cars going north right away, and they send word ahead banana cars are coming. Merchants in different cities come down to the railroad yards and take off as much as they want. They end up in Chicago, and a commission merchant there takes what's left. Now," he added, "I'll tell you a funny thing. I'm not sure it's true but the banana merchants swear it is. All along the railroad lines to Chicago there are men stationed who are called 'banana messengers.' Their job is the unloading of the amount of bananas a merchant specifies. They sleep right alongside the tracks, and the story is that when empty trains go past them their sleep is not disturbed, but let a full train go by, they're awake on the instant, knowing they must get on the job."

Kat said she supposed being a river, the Mississippi was easily navigable, not so complicated as coming into New York harbor where special pilots were required.

I have often noticed, probably because I was born in the Middle West, that people from the East are prone to consider things and people west of the Hudson simple.

Several of the New Orleans folk around us answered simultaneously, one or two of them a little derisively, "I'll have you know," was the theme of their collective answers, "that the mouth of the Mississippi is just about as tricky a spot as a sailor can find anywhere. That's because of the constant shifting of silt. Now you folks in New York can bring ships in with only one additional pilot. Down here it takes two: one the bar pilot and then the river pilot, the bar pilot to get a boat through the mouth and the river pilot to take over. And what's more each one of those is such a special job they can't be traded back and forth. Why, this is something so special it's handed down from generation to generation—bar pilot to bar pilot, river pilot to river pilot. And they don't cross over. No sir!"

Kat found this very interesting, she said. And something she would never have imagined.

"That," I thought to myself, "is the God's truth."

We met more river traffic on the way back than we had encountered earlier, and from the fine, spirited tootings that put a stop to conversation, I doubt there was a boat along our path that did not send us greeting. I was highly gratified by this recognition and pantomimed I would be happy to wave or bow a response but Ellen and Kat by stern gestures of disapproval forbade it. Born in the East they have a restricted behavior pattern.

We came ashore by means of another boat, which seemed to me a novel way of disembarkation. A very large excursion boat was moored at the dock from which we had taken off in the morning, and so our captain landed us alongside the b dock. We moved down our gangplank onto its deck, went across the width of its main saloon, a large and gaily decorated room, came out on its far deck and from there stepped on land.

Mrs. Aldigé drove us back to the hotel though my friends begged her to allow them to walk. They did so want a little fresh air, they said. Considering we had spent the last four hours on the open deck of a yacht, such a craving seemed to Mrs. Aldigé unnatural. She said she'd never heard of such a thing, and would they please get right into the car; they just thought they were putting her out and they weren't one bit. She hadn't another thing in the world to do and wouldn't dream of letting us go back by ourselves.

White-faced and grim-jawed they climbed in. Mrs. Aldigé drove us home, skillfully and carefully. I had not had the slightest doubt she would. I was serene. I could have told my companions the drive out is always the hair-raiser. The drive home is pleasant motoring because the sights of interest have all been taken care of.

Back at the hotel we packed our overnight bags and within an hour were in our own station wagon, on our way to a house in the country. This excursion was a mistake! We saw interesting countryside, unlike any we had seen before. We saw tupelo trees and "poorwill" birds and pelicans riding lovely, deep blue water, and that was that.

ADVICE TO WOMEN TRAVELERS TRAVELING WITH OTHER WOMEN

1. Be a member of the group, not a leader.
2. Do not persuade the rest of them to do something you think they would enjoy.
3. Do not assure them they have been invited to a party just as much as you, when they doubt it.
4. Do not guarantee they will have a wonderful time.
5. Do not operate on the assumption that an extra exuberance on your part will bring together an individual who is your friend and giving the party, and your friends you have brought along.

6. Do not operate on the principle that the stranger who is giving the party is going to be captivated by your anecdotes of the killing things that happened when the members of your group were at school and college together.

v.

7. Do not entertain for a moment the idiotic belief that starting a discussion is a good idea. It starts an argument.

8. Do not reproach your friends for not making it the jolly occasion you had anticipated. They will begin by pointing out your obtuseness in including them in the first place and before they finish they will have enumerated a good many other shortcomings they have observed in you.

9. When the episode is over, do not refer to it again until at least a week after returning from the whole trip. And even then, be careful.

These rules are indispensable when a gentleman is involved. If there is no such involvement they are not worth noticing.

We arrived back in New Orleans in time for lunch. The drive was uninterrupted by sightseeing or conversation. At our hotel, the clerk at the desk told us a lady had arrived, asked for us, and been given a room alongside ours just as we'd asked.

"It's Luz," we said. I added it was the only thing we'd been together on since we'd left New Orleans the day before. Sophy's answer was unqualified. "Thanks to you," she said. I made no further observation.

When we beat noisily on Luz's door, however, we were all talking, welcoming her, and she was answering from the other side. Within a few minutes, and still talking, we were on our way to lunch at an oyster bar. We'd been saving this excursion for her arrival, I told her.

Kat overheard me. "Why not at all," she said, "we haven't had time, and we've been out of town." Kat is unalterably factual.

Felix's Oyster Bar is between Royal and Bourbon Streets, and we found it little short of wonderful. We stood at a bar, a foot on the traditional rail, and though Kat would be all for statistics, I prefer not to set down the number of oysters we ate. We began by ordering half a dozen apiece. Sophy inserted a qualification that gave tone to the group and astonishment to its members. "Cock oysters, please," she said.

We were inclined to be skeptical of such biological discrimination. Sophy appealed to the man behind the bar who was serving us and he gave her full marks.

"Sure, that's right," he said, "cock oysters are sweeter and tenderer, but," he added, "very few foreigners, as you might say, know how to order them."

(For the remainder of that whole day, Sophy was something of a trial to the rest of us, but she eventually came off her high horse and admitted it was Mrs. Stern who had provided her with such superior knowledge.)

Pointing to a stack of clean dishes and an assortment of jars and bottles, the bartender said, "Those are the fixings to make up what suits you," and turned back to Sophy. "I guess I needn't tell you that," he added.

Sophy, rendered by this completely beyond herself, smiled winningly in response and told him, "Oh no, but I prefer only lemon juice. That brings *out* the flavor. I don't like things that take away from it."

The barkeeper smacked the palm of his hand on the counter. "You certainly know your oysters," he told her.

We commoner folk mixed horse radish, catsup, and a little Tabasco into a cocktail sauce to our respective liking, and settled in to silent enjoyment, but Sophy was not yet finished.

"I'd like a beer, too," she requested.

Again her soulmate across the bar was delighted. "Of course you do," he told her. "That's the ticket," and turning his head a little, bawled out into space, "Draw one."

After a consultation as to whether we preferred to expose ourselves again to Sophy's superiority or do without beer, I asked the bartender if we could have four more glasses, please.

"Draw four," he shouted into space and with a quirk of his head toward Sophy added, "She'll tell you what's what."

This was galling but the draught beer was delicious.

For Sophy and me the oysters made a complete lunch and they should have, considering the number we ate. But the rest moved on after the first half dozen to a table in an adjoining room. When Sophy and I joined them some time later, they were just finishing up a gumbo they pronounced wonderful, and were waiting for Kat to have a dessert.

"I want a sweet," she explained.

The rest of us except Luz, the newcomer, joined spontaneously in the chorus we knew now by heart, "To take away the taste of the other food that was delicious."

Our guidebooks were open within five minutes of our leaving the oyster bar. I suppose New Orleanians who go shopping in the French Quarter move directly to the object of their errand and then home again. But for one who does not claim the French Quarter of New Orleans his neighborhood, I count it impossible to walk a straight line along those streets without a sightseeing detour.

The old French Opera House was burned down some years ago, but if you go around the corner from Felix's Oyster Bar onto Bourbon Street, you will see where it stood, because the street unexpectedly widens part way down the block. This was in order for carriages to stop at the very door of the opera. This was where the great plantation owners up and down the Mississippi had come with their wives and families each winter in the opera season. This was where the carnival balls were held.

We stood looking at it, imagining how it must have been in those romantic, ample days. And then we learned from the guide-book that directly opposite had been the Picayune Restaurant of Lafcadio Hearn, a soup kitchen where a man could get a big bowl of good soup for five cents, and that the coin for it in those days was a silver half-dime called a "picayune." I had never before known the source of that word.

We retraced our steps and at the corner of Royal and Iberville Streets, Sophy, who was still considerably above herself, pointed out a big shop on the corner and explained somewhat patroniz-ingly, "That's the famous Solari's. It's one of the great food shops in the country, particularly for Creole specialties. Would you like to go in and see it?"

"I would," Darn answered. "I've got errands there. I have an account at this store. I always keep stocked up with quite a lot of their things and I want to reorder. Do you get things here, too?"

Sophy is always honest. "I've only known about it since last Saturday," she admitted. "Mrs. Stern told me."

I don't know what the others purchased, but I had jars of Creole mustard sent home for myself and my gourmet sons-in-law. I do not know any mustard like it in taste and it proved such a success with my family they have reordered it. The tinned crayfish bisque and shrimp bisque have had the same enthusiastic stamp of approval. I have used the shrimp bisque as soup and also as sauce, as I learned in Louisiana, for boiled fresh shrimp and rice. I, too, now have an account with Solari's, and it is an active one.

More sightseeing again: reading, looking, pointing, exclaim-ing, so enjoying it we protested vehemently Darn's assertion we had barely time to get back to the hotel, freshen up a little and arrive at the hour we'd been asked for cocktails by a friend of

Luz's. It was, of course, characteristic of Darn to be conscious of the passage of time.

On our way to the cocktail party as we left the elevator in our hotel and rounded a corner into the lobby proper, I heard a voice and stopped, restraining the others, too. "Girls," I said (if I may be forgiven the expression), "I haven't heard that voice in five years, but I'll bet you anything you like it's my friend Emma Michie."

We hurried on around the corner and there at the hotel desk stood Emma Michie, all six handsome wonderful feet of her. She had been my hostess and become my friend five years earlier when on a speaking tour I had stayed at the hotel she then owned in Lake Charles. It had been that visit that had nagged me ever since to make the trip now being so richly fulfilled. I had written Emma we would come to Lake Charles and here she was in New Orleans.

"Emma," I shouted, and ran forward to be caught in an embrace that very nearly lifted me off my feet. I recognized another woman standing beside her. At the first sight of Emma anyone in her vicinity is not immediately noticed. "Why," I said, "I remember you in Lake Charles." But I could not at the instant think of her name.

Emma gave me an affectionate nudge in my back. "It's Clara Gebson and she's come with me to take over."

Mrs. Gebson bowed and I thought to myself, either I'm mistaken or she doesn't remember me. But at the same time I thought it unlikely I could have forgotten anyone so extraordinarily pretty, and with such an unusual shade of red-gold hair as genuine as its curl, unless her hairdresser is the greatest in the whole world. However, I did not press my recognition but introduced my friends. Emma acknowledged the introductions with a flood of talk, scarcely noting the names. Clara said, "How do you do?" and nothing more.

I caught up with Emma after her first few sentences that had to do with how long it had taken them to get there and the number of telephone calls she'd been making. "So you see," she was saying, "we decided the best thing to do was just come up here and take over for you all. How are you going to see our country without someone that knows it showing it to you? So a friend of mine has given us his house down at Grand Isle, that's one of the places we're taking you. You can stay there as long as you like. It's right on the Gulf. His cook's all ready to fix you the best food you've ever tasted. Now Williemel's going with us too, because you know she lives in New Orleans but she's lived mostly in Thibodaux and around those parts."

"Whom did you say?" I asked.

"Williemel. Williemel Howell. She's a friend of mine, so I called her up and told her we need her bad. She said she'd just love to come. We'll pick her up in the morning. You going to be ready to go tomorrow morning?"

My friends seemed incapable of speech, but I answered we would indeed be ready. I had begun to grasp the general outline of what we were about to do, but I was relieved to see Darn quietly open her bag, take out notebook and pencil and write down swiftly as Emma talked such specific data as were included.

"Grand Isle first, then back to the country around Thibodaux and Houma and St. Martinville, New Iberia, Lafayette—Rosa's going to be waiting for us in New Iberia."

"I'll explain Rosa later," I interjected to my friends.

"And then after a while we're going to get to Lake Charles."

"Emma," I broke in firmly, "this is wonderful, but you'll have to give us some details."

"Details?" Emma looked at me blankly.

Sophy took advantage of my momentary dam across Emma's speech. "Wouldn't Napoleonville make a good center base for all those places except Grand Isle?" Sophy first, last and always is a map reader.

Mrs. Michie agreed it might be, and would have broken through the dam, but Sophy can be persistent.

"Then what do you say we go back there, stay with the Munsons we enjoyed so much, and make that a kind of springboard for some of these other excursions?"

"Anything you say, girls. Anything you say," was Emma's generous endorsement. And she was off again on her own generous proposals. "You all want we should show you around New Orleans tonight? We've got lots of friends. We could have a fine old time."

We thanked her but told her we had made other engagements not knowing she was coming. She was generous about that, too. "We just want you to have the best old time in the world, whatever way you get it. Now are you happy here in the hotel? Of course you are. You got a big handsome suite like mine?"

Happily, she did not wait for an answer, but called out suddenly to a gentleman approaching her though still quite a little distance away. "Well, hello, hello, I was just going to call you up to tell you I was here. Bless your heart. I guess probably you heard me without me going to the telephone. Come on over here and say hello to these beautiful ladies. But I guess you know 'em all right well by now."

At our obvious mutual lack of recognition, she stared from us to the gentleman who by now had reached and embraced Emma. "Why for heaven's sake, girls, don't you know this man is the manager of this very hotel you're staying in? Why he's the most fascinating man in New Orleans. He's an old friend of mine. I love him to death, I do."

"I've been out of town," he told Emma, and, on hearing our names, "I'm extremely sorry I wasn't here when you came. I just got back. Is there anything I can do for you?"

"Give 'em the best suite you got," Emma interposed.

We checked that instantly and conveyed to the manager we were settled in where we were, and had actually been offered a suite some time after our arrival, but because we were not spending any considerable time had preferred not to change.

"Well, is there anything I can do then?" the manager persisted.

"Yes," I told him, "coat hangers. We've been begging for them ever since we arrived, but we don't seem to be able to attract anyone's attention."

It was not very polite of me, I'm afraid, but it was effective. A few hours later when we had returned from cocktails and dinner, three dozen coat hangers were in my room with the compliments of the manager.

Sophy dined that night with old friends, the Alexander Hilsbergs. He is now the conductor of the New Orleans Symphony but had been for years concert master of the Philadelphia Orchestra where Sophy and I had known him. She brought us word of a wonderful dinner at Galatoire's.

We had not fared so well. We had been led to try an off-the-beaten-track restaurant and felt we had been led astray. We considered the meal pedestrian, and by this time we were accustomed to Olympian standards. We were further disgruntled when Sophy told us of going after dinner with the Hilsbergs to a little pastry shop in St. Peter's Street called Quatres Saisons for a sweet and coffee, both melting in your mouth, she said. And furthermore it was an interesting little spot where people gathered at small tables spending the entire evening over coffee or hot chocolate, pastry, and good talk.

I had heard enough of the delights we had missed and asked how it would be if I telephoned the Munsons in Napoleonville to ask if they could take care of a return visit by our considerably enlarged party. I was told it would be fine if I'd wait until I knew what day I could tell them we'd arrive.

Sophy organized our days from the notes Darn had taken on Emma's proposed and certainly rambling odyssey. Consulting together, Sophy, the executive, and Darn, by now conceded to be her deputy, set Saturday as the night for our arrival in Napoleonville. I put in a call at once. The operator said she would ring me back; there was a little trouble with cut-offs at the moment. She asked my name and I told her. "Is that spelled Kimbreaux?" she asked. I let it go. When she told me she had my party, and a man's voice said "Hello," I plunged immediately into my story. I was afraid we'd be cut off.

"Mr. Munson," I said, "it's Emily Kimbrough and I want to tell you we now number nine—nine women strong—and we want to come back to you. We're going to move in on you on Saturday night, all nine of us. So can you make room? We'll stay two nights anyway, maybe more. I can't tell you how pleased we all of us are, and I hope you are, too."

I did not get an immediate answer and repeated, "We're nine women awfully pleased to be moving in on you and we hope you're pleased too."

A voice answered. It had a slightly tremulous quality, a slight stutter, too, and the accent was not Cajun. "I-I don't reckon I g-got the whole gist of this, m'am," I heard. "You don't mean nine ladies coming here? I don't think I rightly can hear you. I don't know exactly what you want of me for nine ladies."

I said briskly, "I'm only trying to tell you I want you to put us up again."

The voice came back a little stronger, "*Who* going to put you up?"

"*You,*" I repeated, "*You, Mr. Munson.*"

"No *m'am.*" The voice was loud, strong and firm now. "No m'am. This is Tommy talking."

"Tommy who?"

"Tommy," he answered with a shout of pride, "Tommy of Tommy's Bar. That's what I'm owner of, and I got no place in it for any lady at all. So I certainly *cannot* take care of nine."

I sent the Munsons a telegram.

Chapter Nine

We left the next morning, two cars full, and though filling of the two cars at the door of the hotel did not entirely stop traffic passing, it did slow and tie it up considerably. We were finally assorted, with Clara Gebson driving Emma Michie's car, and Emma a passenger in the station wagon. Clara explained that Emma was seldom allowed by her friends to drive her own car, not primarily because she drove too fast, but because she had been known to endeavor to use a field as a highway, either out of absent-mindedness or impatience. Her friends had thought it not so important to probe her motives as to prevent further pathfinding.

I sat beside Clara on the front seat, Mrs. Howell was with Luz in the back. Mrs. Howell had joined us in the lobby of the hotel, overnight bag in hand. I had tried to tell her as we were introduced, and my friends had endorsed my sentiments feelingly, that we were staggered by such generosity as hers, to start off on a trip putting herself to any amount of inconvenience, we were sure, in order to show total strangers her countryside. Mrs. Howell had downed all our protests. It was going to be the greatest fun for her she assured us. She just loved taking a trip on the spur of the moment. She hadn't been away for goodness knows how long, and besides she loved telling all about her part of the country, and most of all she was going to be able to tell us all about her operation. Her friends wouldn't let her talk about it any more, though she hadn't half told them how terrible it had been. Three ministers had come to pray for her, but she'd chased them all away. Only afterward when she got well she had gone round and apologized to them. "And call me Williemel," she added.

We loved Williemel Howell from that instant. Looking at one another surreptitiously our original group members corroborated this.

Williemel took charge immediately and our executive, Sophy, was for once submissive. Williemel said we might get separated in the heavy city traffic, so she'd better set a place on the highway where we'd meet and go on together from there. "There" turned out to be a bowling alley. It was not a spot I would have thought of as a trysting place, but Williemel said you couldn't miss it and she was sure Emma would know it.

Emma, after a moment's reflection, said she knew it very well. They'd had a campaign rally one time there. We were to learn that she is a fervent political campaigner and that the Huey Long regime had been given a powerful push down by her hand.

On our way to the bowling alley I ventured to broach to Clara the matter of identity that had been bothering me ever since our introduction the night before. "Mrs. Gebson," I began a little shyly, *"didn't* I meet you in Lake Charles when I was there? And weren't we together quite a few times?"

Clara, driving, put her head down on the wheel for a brief instant. And when she raised it again I could see she was blushing a little. "I feel such a fool," she said, "but it was those white gloves you all were wearing. You looked so dressed up and I felt so dirty and grubby from the car, I just couldn't bear to shake hands with you so I pretended I didn't know you at all. I'm truly sorry. I don't know what got into me."

I reassured her. "It's Darn's white gloves," I told her. "You'll get used to them in time. We don't know why they always look whiter than anyone else's, but they do. She always wears them, and they never are the least bit dirty. Maybe she carries spares in pockets on various parts of her."

Williemel interrupted. "Now we're passing a store," she said, "I want you to take notice of because it's got a right cute story about it." She pointed to a large market we were passing at the moment on the Airline Highway and I read the name, Schwegmann's. "It's a wonderful place and they sell things cheaper than anybody else and that makes the other merchants mighty mad, but that's not the reason it's so cute. The reason is the family that runs it. Sons and father, goodness knows who all. Father's on a trip abroad and if you please, the store runs full-page ads in the *Times Picayune* and prints in the ads the letters he is writing home to his family. They think everybody's interested in poppa's trip, and we are."

Later I saw some of the advertisements and the letters, and I was interested, too. I read about poppa's sojourn in Holland, the famous pictures he had seen and the ones he liked; what he thought about the inconvenience of going through customs in European countries, and his reports on European merchandising methods. All of this encircled by sales items of garbage-pan covers, bathroom heaters, oysters, onions, gold belt buckles, fruitcake ingredients, and among the many other items one I had not known about: piggie patties, for turkey stuffing. I shall not forget Schwegmann's advertisement.

We found the bowling alley without any difficulty. It was indeed well marked with a good deal of neon. The establishment included a gas station, and while Clara had the car checked, Luz and I got out, walked to the rim of the highway to look for and flag the other car. A considerable time passed. We were becoming anxious and were discussing the possibility of leaving a message with the gas attendant, in case they should arrive, telling them to stay. Meantime we would go back and retrace our steps in the hope of finding some clue to their whereabouts, when we heard a tattoo sounded on the horn and the station wagon drove in.

Emma Michie had been the cause of their delay and she was the first to acknowledge it with some pride. "I took them in the wrong direction," she called out before the car had come to a stop. "I told them nobody should ever pick on me to show the way because that's something I never know. But I wouldn't even have known it was the wrong way if Sophy hadn't asked me did I think we were going right and I said, No, I didn't think we were. So then she said maybe we'd better turn around, and look at us, right where we said we'd be. I told you we'd find you all, didn't I?"

"We're off to see the wizard," we sang, and we were on our way again.

We took Route 90 to Raceland, where we stopped a few minutes to watch enormous trucks, a dozen or so, heaped to overflowing with cane and lined up along the approach to a mill. We turned south there taking Route 308, and we were, we suddenly discovered, riding along beside the Bayou Lafourche. We discovered it simultaneously. Sophy blew her horn a rapid staccato and I waved and pointed out my window.

I was excited. "This is what I've been talking about ever since I went to Lake Charles," I said, "I'll never forget being driven from there to a speaking date in Beaumont, Texas, and riding along the road, seeing suddenly a boat of considerable size that seemed to be floating in the middle of a meadow. I'd looked away and then back again to make sure it wasn't a mirage or an aberration. And then I asked my companion who was driving me if that could possibly be a boat moving in a meadow. And she said it was a boat but not in a meadow, it was on a bayou, and that a bayou wasn't like a river, it didn't have steep banks approaching it, but was level with the land on either side; so if that land had high vegetation on it, you couldn't see the water from even a short distance away."

I knew as I was telling this I was conveying no remarkable information to my companions, to whom a bayou was no novelty. Even Luz had at least visited this part of the country many times. I knew all this but I wanted to say aloud my deep pleasure in the literal fulfillment of something I had so hopefully told my other friends would be as I'd remembered it.

In the very act of my saying this aloud, a piercing halloo from Sophy's horn told me they saw on the instant what I was looking at around the bend ahead of us. The shrimp fleet was coming in, moving toward us in the sunlight through meadows, and presently we could read their names, *Five Daughters, Southern Belle, Two Sons, Evening Star, Only Son* and more. We saw their nets festooned for drying. We saw their white hulls and bright trimmings, red, blue, green, pink and yellow.

The bayou is broad and that morning it was heavy with traffic; little tugs strutting through the water drawing a line of barges behind, large boats that bore along the hull the name of an oil company and top-heavy with cumbersome machinery.

Along the side of the road away from the bayou, Williemel pointed out to us mud ovens outside trim little cottages we passed. "The women bake once a week in those ovens," she told us and said again what Mr. Munson had insisted, that they were all thrifty people and prosperous. Daughters in these families were provided with "dots" that would not make a family ashamed. When I wondered aloud that so much substance could be earned from such small plots of ground, Williemel told us that though these were closely populated settlements, or seemed so from the road, the land ran back behind each house in narrow strips for a considerable acreage. The houses themselves were not weather-beaten shacks such as we had seen with Mr. Munson. They were small but well-built cottages and all of them attractively painted. The lawns were well kept and fenced, and each property included a flower garden.

"They're really wonderful people," Williemel said. "They haven't had much education but you'd like to think your children had the manners theirs have. You know these families are descendants of some of the finest in France and Spain. This immediate section was settled by younger sons, and don't tell me heredity doesn't show. Why you can go this day to one of the littlest cottages and you'll be offered hospitality, a cup of coffee, a glass of wine, maybe just a glass of water, but with a manner that'd make you think you're being received at court. And that makes me think," she added, hopefully, "when I was recovering from my operation and had visitors . . ."

But I interrupted her. "Don't you want to tell us when we're all together?" And I added, "I'm hungry. What would you say to looking for a place to eat?"

Williemel was easily diverted. Clara and Luz backed my suggestion enthusiastically. We began looking for a restaurant and presently saw advertisements of the Huba-Huba Café, indicating its location a few miles farther on. The signs were repeated at intervals, but I was inclined to be dubious of a café with such a name.

"It sounds like a roadhouse to me," I said, "and I don't think we'd get very good food in such a place in the middle of the day."

Williemel disputed this. "You'll get good food in this part of the country any time of the day and pretty much anywhere. I say we chance it."

I am grateful to Williemel for more things than I could enumerate on a full page, but at the top of the list would be the Huba-Huba Café at Golden Meadows. It isn't for the food alone I would headline it, though the shrimp gumbo we ate would justify such headlining, but for the very place itself.

Sophy drew in just behind us and her car was emptied quickly and enthusiastically when I called out that food was the reason for our stopping. But like me they were dubious about the place itself.

"All right," Williemel told us, "if we don't like it we can turn around and walk out."

We did not walk out for two hours.

We went into a room with a bare wooden floor and walls, and at the far end a bar. The proprietor, tending it, was surprised by an invasion of nine women, but too courteous to display it other than by an involuntary start as we poured in. The next instant he had come from behind the bar, and introducing himself, was pushing tables together, welcoming us in French and English, urging us to have shrimp just off the boat and suggesting with thoughtful candor that probably first of all we would like to go to the bathroom. But when we immediately accepted his last suggestion, he summoned his daughter from the kitchen, introduced her, and then ordered her not to take us to the room but simply to point out the location. This seemed to me a delicate distinction.

A waiter or headwaiter in any restaurant would have quailed, I am sure, at the necessity of sorting out the orders of nine women, independent women, too, all chattering at once. But not the proprietor of this restaurant. "Take the gumbo," he said, and we did.

While we waited for lunch to come, Williemel seized the opportunity to begin the narrative of her operation. That is, she tried. But before she could so much as take us with her to the hospital, Clara and Emma distracted us by the stories of their campaigning for Governor Jones in the downfall of Huey Long— not only the meetings at which Clara or Emma had spoken, but the meetings the intrepid Emma had created from a group of Cajuns gathered at a bar or in a dancehall.

"They were right confused at first," Clara said, "but pretty soon other people would come in and join them and Emma'd keep right on talking. You can't stop Emma talking, not without your putting considerable effort into it."

This I counted an understatement.

Williemel came back to us from the hospital with anecdotes about the people hereabouts and Clara and Emma gave way. This time Williemel was not talking about the Cajuns but about her friends in and around Thibodaux. We would call on "Miss" Bessie Shaeffer she promised us. Maybe she wouldn't be at home but we'd at least see her house. It was a beautiful antebellum place and had been lived in by the same family for over a hundred years. I was momentarily startled to hear her grandchildren referred to, though I know "Miss" is a courtesy title of the region.

When lunch arrived and was being served, Williemel had passed "Miss" Bessie and her house and was telling us about a wonderful old character in the vicinity, a colored man who was a local gardener working for everyone around about and more than a gardener, a true horticulturist, deeply respected for his knowledge by everyone who knew him and that covered a wide range.

Williemel chuckled. "He makes the men kind of mad, though," she explained. "Every year on Mother's Day he sends their wives flowers. But the first of the following month the husbands get a bill for them. And what makes those men really mad is that most of them forget to send any themselves."

Kat stiffened. "I should think they would be mad," she said sharply. "My husband certainly wouldn't care to have any man send me flannels on Mother's Day or any other time."

Luz was sitting across the table. She leaned forward and spoke carefully and with exaggerated articulation. "Flowers, dear; Williemel said flowers, not flannels."

Two things happened simultaneously; a bottle of beer was set down in front of each of us and we acknowledged with lifted glasses Luz's position in the group. She was, we toasted her, official interpreter and liaison between accents. I had noticed in the few hours she had been with us how malleable her own accent was, not crisp with her old friends, Luz could never be crisp, but each word detached from the word before it, and occasionally she exposed an "r." But let Louisiana folk admit us to their circle and Luz slid her words and "r's" to join their accent, all the while keeping a watchful and protective eye on us, ready to keep clear all avenues of verbal communication, and communication of ideas.

Williemel, lifting her glass, said it. "They talk so fast sometimes, and I know we talk too easy. Luz, you're just wonderful for both of us."

We bent to our gumbos and after that there was very little conversation, either fast or easy.

When we had finished lunch we explored the rest of the restaurant. From where we sat we had caught a glimpse of a room beyond and sounds of voices there. We found that room to have a dance floor and also a bar at its far end. But in an alcove of the room some ten or twelve men were gathered at a big round table playing cards. We immediately asked if we might watch, and they shyly but hospitably said we might. They were shrimp men, we learned, just off their boats. They were almost all of them handsome and all of them very brown with aquiline noses, black eyes and hair.

"It's *bourré* they're playing," Williemel said.

One of the men, hearing her, laughed and showing startlingly white teeth said, "*C'est ça. Bourré.*"

None of us had the faintest idea of the game so it was difficult to follow, but fun to watch. Not much money was being exchanged, mostly dimes, quarters, fifty-cent pieces; but there was a considerable amount of excitement, and such rapid speech, all of it French, of course, that we could catch only an occasional word. I could have stayed another hour or even more listening, but Williemel urged us to move along or we wouldn't reach Grand Isle before dusk.

"The way you all like to stop and look at things, I've got a feeling we just won't keep going," she said.

As I was getting into the car I saw something take place in the station wagon that stopped me motionless for an instant and then brought me backing out and on the run to peer dismayed through the front window to see Sophy sitting on the *right* side of the front seat. "Are you ill?" I demanded anxiously, and looked beyond her at Luz behind the wheel.

Sophy smiled. "Not at all," she assured me. "Luz is the only woman I know I would drive with. She's taking over. I'm just going to enjoy myself."

Darn folded her hands in her lap, her white gloves gleaming. "In this group," she observed, "no one feels superior very long. Enjoy it, Luz, while you can."

I went back to my car.

Williemel had been right. In less than an hour after leaving the Huba-Huba Café we had drawn up to the side of the road again.

We had left the bayou and the little settlements now, and were driving through treeless country with flat meadows on either side stretching all the way to the horizon.

"Those aren't cane fields," I had said to Williemel. "What are they?"

"They're not fields at all, honey," was her answer, "they're marshes. Down here they're called *flottants,* and I can tell you they float all right. If you or I were to step out onto that land we'd be down to our waists or over our heads in a few feet. But this is the trapper's gold mine. He knows every tuft he can put his foot on."

I asked what they trapped.

"Muskrats, mostly," she said. "But I heard there's a funny thing been happening around here recently. It seems somebody got the idea to try raising some nutria, so he got himself a few pairs and started breeding them in captivity. But the pesky things got out. Well, the men that were doing the breeding thought that was the end of that, but next thing anybody knew there were nutria around, and then there were more of them. Those animals hadn't been swallowed up, they had taken over. Now they tell me there are great quantities of them. But the trappers have to use different methods for getting them than they use on muskrats. And these trappers don't like anything that's different. So what's going to happen beween the muskrats and the nutria I don't rightly know. But this much I can tell you, and anybody'll bear me out on it. Louisiana catches and sells more animals to the fur industry than all the rest of the United States put together."

She interrupted herself with a sudden exclamation. "Look at that over there. Slow down, Clara." Clara obeyed instructions and Williemel, leaning forward, pushed her arm through the open window beside Clara and waved a forefinger animatedly. "You see that hump over there that looks something like a cross between a beehive and a haystack?"

It took me a minute or two to train my eye on the center of the loops and circles her finger was describing, but suddenly I saw in that silent, monotonous stretch of marsh land a hump, bigger than, but as round as a beehive, and smaller than a hay-stack. "That's a muskrat house," she said. "It's like an apartment. It's got two stories. Isn't that wonderful? And look down there ahead," her finger made whorls again. "There's a trapper's hut. Let's go call on the people there."

That was where we stopped.

A weatherbeaten shack alongside of the road was separated from it by a little bayou, bridged from the roadside to the doorstep of the shack by two wooden planks.

When the passengers from the station wagon joined us, I explained what we had been seeing and where we were about to go. By the time I had finished, two women had appeared in the doorway of the little shack and were eying us with friendly curiosity. One was very old, thin and shrunken. She wore a clean but faded cotton dress and a big sunbonnet on her head. Standing beside her was a taller woman, heavy set, with brown hair and weatherbeaten tanned face.

We hadn't realized until we left the cars that a considerable wind had sprung up. We felt it standing on the road, but as we started in single file across the wooden planks, we were considerably impeded by it. It blew our skirts up and tight around us, threatened our balance, none too steady at best on those wooden planks, and caused Emma and Williemel to squeal and protest every step their inability to go forward or go back. But we did all of us arrive without mishap and crowded around the threshold of the little shack.

We were welcomed exactly as Williemel had told us we would be in this part of the country, with complete self-possession and dignity. The younger of the two women invited us to enter as though a visitation of this sort were an everyday occurrence.

We moved into a little room with bare floor, shining clean, an iron bedstead in one corner with beautiful patchwork quilt as a throw and spotless but coarse linen sheet turned down over the top of it. In the other corner of the room were a wooden and canvas frame and open burlap bags that held strips of material. The old lady explained that making rugs was her occupation. The younger one introduced the old lady as her mother, said her husband was a trapper out looking over the land, because the trapping season would not open for another few days, but they were getting ready for it. Her husband's name, she said, was Leon Cheramie. We introduced ourselves and she introduced her mother, Mme. Melançon. Both of them spoke only French,

and when I say good French, I mean French we could understand.

Mme. Melançon asked if we had come from any distance. We said New York. She nodded her head. She herself had once visited a large city, Biloxi, by name, she said. She had not cared for it though the stores had been handsome. However, she had found too much noise and confusion and futhermore it had rained that day. So she had been glad to return home and had not traveled since. She supposed New York was like Biloxi. Very much like it, we told her.

I asked her daughter if muskrats were what her husband trapped. She said not entirely. He also, like other trappers, got otter and mink.

It was a delightful visit and we told our hostesses how much we had enjoyed their hospitality. They hoped, politely, we would drop in again one day, if we happened by from New York. We assured them we would be delighted.

Presently we were on the long causeway that leads to Grand Isle, and all along this part of the country we pointed out to one another kingfishers, blue heron and white, and the ubiquitous pelican, absurd creatures that were a constant delight to me. The air was cold, the afternoon was getting on, the sky was gray

and the wind blew harder. We left the causeway and we were on Grand Isle proper, narrow, with scant vegetation, not unlike the parts of the New Jersey coast I have known. Down the one main road a mile or so, and we were at the house we were to occupy. Clara blew her horn, Luz followed with a signal from hers. A man and woman came from the house, the woman smiling, waving, very stout, dressed in slacks and a blouse open at the throat. The man was small and very thin; both of them were hospitable, friendly.

They spoke no English but they shouted in French, "Go quickly, go quickly, come back later. We take your bags. The shrimp boats are coming in. The shrimp boats are coming in!"

Chapter Ten

THE SHRIMP BOATS WERE DOCKED WHEN WE REACHED the landing. As we opened the doors of our cars we could hear a jumble of men's voices, women's too; machinery and hurrying footsteps. We ran around the corner of a long gray wooden shed that separated us from the boat and were on a wide wooden walk that edged the water. The walk was very wet; there was a good deal of ice in small pieces scattered about. We slowed down in order not to slip on the surface.

"Oh dear," Ellen said, "I wish they could begin all over again. I don't know which way to look."

I agreed with her. I didn't know myself where to begin looking. On my left through the open doors of the shed I could see women working busily at something. Immediately ahead of us, a little boy, perhaps twelve years old, was guiding and pushing great masses of shrimp with a shovel along a chute that emptied into the shed. On my right big baskets were being lowered by a crane into the hold of the boat nearest me, and returning to the surface brimming with shrimp and small pieces of ice that spilled and scattered along the walk at our feet.

I walked over to the edge and looked down where the crane was operating. I found myself looking into the upturned face of as handsome a young man as I have seen in many a day. He was standing, feet wide apart, up to his knees and over in shrimp. His face was a glowing brown, his eyes were dark, his hair black and curly. He laughed at my start of astonishment. I had expected to see shrimp, but not a man knee-deep in them. His teeth were strong, white and even. He was as French in type as any fisherman bringing in his catch off the coast of Normandy.

"*Bonjour,*" he said, and still in French, "You have come, perhaps, to see a few shrimp?"

We both laughed at that.

I told him I'd like to see everything, but at the moment I could see he was a little busy. And we laughed again. I would go watch what else was happening and perhaps I could come back a little later and talk to him. He assured me he would be delighted to receive me. This was his boat. He would like to show it all to me, and would like me to meet his wife, who was on board. Probably he did not accompany this speech with a courtly bow over the shrimp and ice below him, but certainly that was the gesture he suggested by the courtliness of his manner and speech. We said "*À bientôt*" to each other and I turned to go away but stopped and asked if I might take his picture. It was so late in the afternoon, I doubted, I told him, I could get a successful one, but I'd like to try. He was delighted with the idea and stopped filling a basket to stand motionless for me. It's a picture I treasure, that vivid young man laughing up from a mound of shrimp around him.

I left him and visited next the little boy shoveling the catch down the trough. I have his picture, too, and he is every bit as handsome as the young man in the hold: close-cropped black curly hair, brown face, big dark eyes. They are wonderful-looking people.

Our group had scattered. I found some of them inside the shed and joined them to watch, across a trough, a line of women. Their hands were moving so swiftly I could not, for a minute or two, discover what they were doing. The trough between them and me was the continuation of the one at which the little boy had been working, filled with running water and bits of ice. Some of the young women wore rubber gloves, others worked with their bare hands, purple from the cold water.

I thought at first the process was the separating of shrimps for size, but after keeping my attention fixed on one pair of hands,

I realized they were removing the heads. The women, and they were for the most part young, and also good-looking, swept into each hand a fistful of shrimp as they floated by, and with each thumb flicked off the heads, opened their hands, released those beheaded and scooped up another fistful.

I walked the length of the trough and found at the other end the shrimp being reloaded into baskets, the heads separated into other containers, the baskets of shrimps weighed and then loaded into one of a number of tremendous trucks backed to the landing platform; and I saw that the trucks themselves were refrigerated.

A man was standing by the scales on which the baskets were being weighed and their weight written on a chart by two workers. He was the only one in the shed who seemed not to be working under pressure, but supervising, and I ventured to talk to him. I was not surprised to find him cordial, hospitable to our coming, not particularly surprised by it, though I doubt a sudden in-tide of nine women is a daily occurrence, but like every single person we encountered he had beautiful manners. He spoke partly in French partly in English and told me how the boats went out with their holds filled with ice, that the shrimp from the moment of being caught were never without refrigeration, that they worked at top speed in the unloading in order to finish before dark and get the trucks on their way to the city and their further transportation.

I asked how they knew when to get the trucks and the workers ready at the shed. And what he told me had a flavor I found as delectable as that of the shrimp itself. Every boat, he said, was equipped with all kinds of modern engineering aids including a ship-to-shore telephone. The captains telephoned that the boats were coming in; they always came in by agreement, at the same time, so no one had advantage over another. Immediately a man on duty in the shed got the news, he didn't telephone, he didn't push a button or flash an electric signal of some sort; he ran outside and pulled the rope of a great hand bell. The sound of that bell was a signal to the village that the fleet was coming in, and from out the cottage doors the girls came running, the drivers of the trucks left their games of *bourré,* or whatever, and drove to the shed, and everything was in readiness when the boats sailed into view. Sometimes the fleet would have been gone a week, sometimes a few days, depending of course on the catch and the weather. But by ship-to-shore and then by a kind of town crier sounding the alarm, everyone was on hand for its arrival.

The workers at the scale interrupted politely to ask something about the truck loading, and I said I would not bother my informant any longer, but might I look about a little more? He urged me to do this and to board the *Bienvenue.* It was a fine boat, he said, and pointed out the window to the one I had photographed.

On my way back through the shed I gathered up Ellen, Luz and Sophy. The others were not in sight. I told them we'd been invited to board the *Bienvenue.* We walked out to the dock and saw its name brightly painted along the bow. We climbed on board and were greeted immediately by the captain's wife, who'd been told, she said, we were coming.

She was small, pretty, as fair as he was dark, and spoke not a word of English. She had with her their son, a chubby, very blond little Cajun about six years old. He was dressed in a Roy Rogers suit. His name, his mother told us, was Pierre. Pierre Cheramie, but they called him "Beelee." The name was the same as the trapper's we had met, I told her. She said they were relatives.

We left Beelee practicing with his lariat from the deck to a bulkhead, and followed Mme. Cheramie. She took us first to the bridge, the forecastle, whatever that place is called from which a boat is operated; I am not versed in nautical terms. Her husband joined us there. He showed us a magnificent panel and explained the purpose of each lever and button. But since I am not better at engineering than I am at nautical terms, and furthermore since it was all done in French, my understanding of what he told us was a bit cloudy. But I was deeply impressed.

I do remember there was an automatic pilot, and there was an instrument for determining the depth of water and the location of shrimp, but I could even be mistaken about that. I could not

be mistaken about his pride in his boat. That needed no termi-
nology; it was evident in the way he smoothed the panel with the
palm of his hand and patted the gleaming woodwork around it.
But within a few minutes he asked politely if we would excuse
him. He must get back to the unloading.

When he had gone, Mme. Cheramie told us his family had
been shrimp fishermen for generations. He had been in the last
war and when he had got out had designed this boat and had
it built by his brother-in-law. It had cost him $47,000 but he was
a hard worker and had paid it off in a year and a half. This, I
thought, was hard work that paid off well. She went on to say that
he averaged about $1,200 for five days' to a week's fishing, but
that of course the two men who worked with him had to be paid
out of that. I still considered it a good reward for hard work.

Sophy asked if she went with her husband on the fishing trips;
Mme. Cheramie shuddered. Never, she said, though her family,
too, had always been shrimp fishermen. She herself disliked boats
very much. She'd only come on board to cook supper for him.
They lived in Golden Meadow a few miles away, but when she
got a telephone call he was coming in, she always came over to
prepare supper for him so that no time would be lost in the
unloading.

She led us back to the galley, pausing on the way to show
us the men's sleeping quarters—comfortable and spotlessly clean.
On the stove in the galley, and the galley was shining neat, a
large iron pot was three-quarters filled with something boiling
and bubbling. To the right of it on a shelf let down from the
wall were strips of wax paper, and at the left on a stool a deep
covered dish.

"We eat shrimp tonight," our hostess said.

I asked if they always ate shrimp.

"Oh no," she told me, and laughed. "That would be too much.
But today is Friday."

She dropped into the bubbling liquid, which I realized was
deep fat, a long-handled strainer, brought it up filled with golden
brown shrimp. She emptied these onto the wax paper and turning

to us asked timidly, "Do you, perhaps, like the shrimp? I hope you will eat."

I could scarcely answer her. My eyes were streaming with an involuntary reaction of yearning for those lovely things. My salivary glands were working at such a pitch I had to swallow several times before I could become articulate enough to assure her I liked them very much indeed, and would be happy to try one or two if it were not depriving them.

This time she laughed as loud and as spontaneously as a child. "You do not deprive us," she assured me. "I think you will agree we have enough."

We joined her laughter when Luz observed she did not believe even my capacity would exhaust the tonnage we had seen coming from the hold.

There is no use hoping that ever in my life I will taste more glorious food than those shrimp, dipped from the sea to a bed of ice in the hold of a boat, from there to a kettle and from that kettle straight to me. I do not know that I even *want* to hope for anything more glorious. I like better to remember how it was that late afternoon when I reached forward and picked up by the tail a shrimp so fresh and so hot I had to wave it a few times in the air before I could put my teeth into its firm sweetness. It had been rolled in a very thin batter, I discovered, as I savored its beauty, and it needed no seasoning.

I am dishonest when I refer to what I ate as "it." Like the man in the song, "You first take one, and then take two, and then you don't care what you do." I took one and then two, and would not then have cared whether I ever ate anything else, had I not suddenly remembered that the cook back at the house who had hurried us off to see the docking had called after us, "Dinner will be waiting when you come back." I thought, too, in a dreamy, far-off way of the days and weeks of Ry-Krisp and lettuce that awaited me in New York at the end of this trip. This was a thought that had a habit of recurring during the trip, but I had become skillful in suppressing it before it overshadowed my pleasure. This time, however, I drew back my hand from one more shrimp, reluctantly told my hostess I thought we must leave.

The others, who are more moderate than I about food, and it exasperates me, had already withdrawn, but joined me in thanking our hostess for providing an experience we would never forget.

On deck Beelee was still practicing with his lariat, and as we climbed down again to the dock, *Monsieur le Capitaine* hailed us from the hold and we bent down to call to him our thanks. The pile of shrimp had been decreased until it was now only around his ankles. I told him what a marvelous supper was waiting for him; we had sampled it.

"My wife is a good cook," he assured us. "She makes everything fine."

I told him I could well believe that, and we waved good-by.

We found the rest of our group at another shrimp boat along the line. We called them, and as they came toward us Williemel pointed to a large bag Emma was carrying, and pantomimed it was shrimp given from the boat *they* had visited.

As we were closing the doors of the station wagon, someone shouted and we looked out. Hurrying toward us was the gentleman with whom I had talked in the shed. He carried in each arm a sack of such size that each arm barely reached around it, and he was a little out of breath when he came up to us. "You must not go," he said, "without some shrimp," and held out both the bags.

Emma, who was riding with us for the return trip, hastily put both feet across and spread her skirt around the bag she had been carrying and had placed on the floor beside her. She reached out her arms for first one bag and then the other of the new batch. "Why," she said, "that's just wonderful. I was hoping we might have a few little fresh shrimp right off the boats. This is certainly kind of you. I'm Emma Michie from Lake Charles."

I was learning that in this part of the country one must immediately establish one's identity but I had not as yet quite got the knack of knowing when to insert the information.

The gentleman, putting in the second bag with some little difficulty because Emma could not move over to make place for it since she had the original loot clamped between her feet, introduced himself at once. He was Monsieur Brignac, the owner of the Circle Shrimp Company for which all these boats operate. He assured us he would have regretted it always had he allowed us to leave without the compliments of the Circle Shrimp Company. We exchanged handshakes, bows all around, and reiterating our gratitude finally drove off.

Darn thought it might be a good idea to bury one of the bags of shrimp before we reached the house, lest the cook, confronted with such a quantity, walk out and leave us with them. But Kat was appalled at the very thought of such waste. We were glad her opinion had been the deciding one, because the cook, though not overjoyed, did not suggest leaving. "I cook some of them," she said, "although I have prepared shrimp, of course, but these I will boil as an extra, and the rest I can put in the deep freeze."

The words "deep freeze" she said in English, and Kat observed as she got out of the car, "Thank goodness I'm beginning to understand their French."

In our haste on our arrival we had not stepped inside the house, but we explored it now and were immediately enthusiastic. We were still dazed by the hospitality and generosity of people in the South. Here a man in Lake Charles, hearing of totally strange women who wanted to tour the country, would open his house, staff it and stock it with every comfort. Under such astonishing circumstances we would have been grateful for a rude cabin. Instead, we found ourselves in a comfortable, large cottage.

From the doorway we looked straight across a center living-dining room to a door with window top that gave us a view of beach and, beyond it, the Gulf of Mexico. The first thing we did was cross the room, open that door and walk out over a broad screened porch, out another door on its far side, and stand with the wind beating our skirts around us, while we looked over a great stretch of water and white beach between. We didn't stay long, the wind was too strong. When we had re-entered the house we peeked in at two bedrooms on the first floor and then climbed to the second to find a center hall corresponding to the main room below, and of such dimensions as to make it an extra living room, furnished as such. On either side a bedroom and a bath like the ones downstairs, and across the whole front above the screened porch, a dormitory, screened too, and furnished with a row of beds. The dormitory ran not only the full front of the house but along one side. All of us could have slept along that row, and still there would have been beds to spare. But we didn't. I chose an upstairs inside bedroom because, I admitted shame-facedly, I could not go to sleep at night without reading first, and that would certainly be disturbing to the other occupants of the dormitory.

Emma, Clara and Williemel elected to use the downstairs bed-rooms. The rest of us settled on the second floor. Sophy opened her shoebag, and we invited the downstairs residents to join us.

Emma did not come with them. Emma, we learned, does not care for even the proximity of such things as Sophy brought in her shoebag, and prefers to be out of their neighborhood. Emma likes a good earthy story and tells it. She enjoys a hearty com-panionship with all folk and is indulgent of all their foibles save one. Her lips tighten, her eyes that are usually alive with humor grow cold and narrow at the sight or mention of a glass with some-thing alcoholic in it. She says no word of criticism, she just wants no part of it.

When we had finished our moderate but warming sociability upstairs, we came down to find the cook dishing up at the stove in the kitchen that opens without doors from the main room. In the middle of the kitchen on a low chair, Emma sat dressed in a beautiful, lacy, long-flowing tea gown, rocking violently back and forth, talking to the cook in a mixture mostly English with a few strange words thrown in, that I think Emma thought were French, but that the cook must have understood because she was laughing heartily. And as I watched them, the cook put down the dish she was filling, to give Emma a hearty hug. Emma caught sight of us, over the cook's shoulder, and patting the cook's arm released herself, rose slowly from the low rocker, and with great dignity, the tea gown trailing behind her, moved to the head of the table.

The dinner we ate that night would demand, my conscience told me, about an extra week of Ry-Krisp and lettuce. I told my conscience that seemed little enough to pay for such pleasure, and went on eating. In the center of the table was an enormous bowl of boiled shrimp. We took handfuls of them, peeled off the shells, dipped them in butter and lemon juice. After that we ate shrimp gumbo with rice and then broiled speckled trout, delicate and sweet, *petit pois* and green salad.

When the table had been cleared and coffee served, Williemel proposed, "Now if we can find some cards and some chips, I'll teach you all to play *bourré*."

We could find both with no difficulty. They were on the shelf of an open cupboard in the main room. "Bound to be here," Emma said. "Ed uses this cottage mostly for fishing. He brings big parties of men down, and you can believe wherever there are big parties of men, there'll be cards and poker chips. Just look around."

We hadn't heard until now the name of the owner of this camp. "Why it's Ed Taussig," Emma said in answer to my startled observation that we hadn't even asked. "Ed Taussig owns the Ford agency in Lake Charles."

From the tone of Emma's voice I felt I ought to apologize that in New York I had not known of Mr. Taussig, and indeed I assured her I did regret not having known him.

We settled around the dining-room table. Each took an allotment of chips. Williemel shuffled the cards and began. "Now I'm going to tell you all how we play this game."

I have not the slightest idea how the game of *bourré* goes. We played round after round of it, but with each hand Williemel remembered a rule she had not thought of before, or a variation of one she had already given. This did not in the least mar our hilarious enjoyment of the evening, nor our spirited participation in the game, but it did render impossible bringing it back as something new to introduce to our friends at home. Personally, I prefer to return and play it with Williemel. She gives it variety. But the one who ended the evening with all but a few of the chips in neat piles before her was our gatherer of statistics, our conservative New Englander, our dear Kat.

Chapter Eleven

NEXT MORNING, I CAME DOWN THE LAST AS USUAL, TO breakfast conversation about the soothing-to-sleep sound of water rolling in and out, up on the sand and back again.

I injected a contribution, "I wasn't entirely soothed by the sight of fire way out on the water. I could see it from my window. I think the rest of you were asleep because I read for quite a long time. I thought of waking you and giving an alarm that a ship was burning, but then I decided maybe it was just something natural to this country. If boats coast through meadows and vegetable gardens grow above your head on a levee, maybe a fire in the Gulf of Mexico is just run of the mill, too."

Williemel answered me. "Lord, honey," she said, "I certainly wouldn't have thanked you for waking me up to point out an old oil platform."

"An oil platform?" I echoed.

"That's what we call it. It's an oil field out there. An oil rig. It's in operation day and night. It's eight miles out. So it looks just a speck in the daytime, but at night you can see it plain."

Emma chimed in. "That nice young fellow on the shrimp boat yesterday, what was his name?"

"Paul Martin?" Clara suggested.

"That's right. Well, Paul, he was the captain of the boat we were on while you all were on the other, you know what I mean?"

We said we did.

"Well, he was talking about those off-shore drilling rigs. He said they interfered with their shrimping in a bad way. They didn't use to have to go out nearly so far. But now they go thirty-five to forty miles."

Clara broke in. "Why, he told me they went out this time only fifteen miles."

"I don't care if he did," was Emma's answer. "He said plenty of times they've got to go thirty-five to forty to get those jumbo shrimps."

Ellen said reflectively, "You know, we didn't see yesterday any of those little tiny shrimp we get sometimes at home. Are they the babies? I meant to ask you at the time."

Williemel snorted. "Those aren't baby anything, honey. They're just little old river shrimp. Why, these people wouldn't even be bothered with them. Lord, they go all the way down to the Gulf without even noticing them. And you know that's quite a trip. That captain we were talking to. What'd you say his name was, Clara? He was mighty cute looking."

"Martin," Clara said, "Paul Martin. And listen to me just a minute. People in my part consider those little tiny river shrimp a great delicacy. You only get them in the spring."

"That's right, but I'm talking about round here. Don't go confusing these visitors with your Northern talk." She turned to me. "Clara spends a lot of time in Lake Charles, but she lives in Shreveport." Clara, banished to her outpost, subsided but Williemel continued, "Well, Paul told me it takes them four hours to get down to the mouth of the Mississippi. 'Lord,' I told him, 'don't I know? That's where my husband and I used to go fishing. Seemed to me it took us forever to get down there.'"

"How fast do those boats go?" Kat wanted to know. She always extracts statistics out of any conversation.

Clara answered her. "I don't know how fast they can go, but Paul said when they get the nets set then they only travel five miles an hour."

"I should think," Kat commented, "that when he told you that you'd have asked him what the boat's top speed was."

"Me?" Clara said. "Why it wouldn't have done any good if I had, because I wouldn't have got it straight nor remembered it.

I never pay any attention to figures anyway. How high is something, how deep is something, how fast can we go? All those numbers? I just can't stand to look at them, and I don't want anybody to talk to me about them."

Probably blasphemy would have shocked Kat more than this utterance, but not much.

I jumped into the conversation. "Williemel," I began, "did you say you'd gone fishing around here? Is it good fishing?"

The spontaneous hoots that greeted this inquiry of mine startled our Southern friends. But Luz explained that the picture of me participating in any sport had overwhelmed my friends. "Forget about Emily," she added to Williemel. "Just tell me. I'm the one that loves such things."

"Well, you see," Williemel answered her, "we had a cottage here for years."

We hadn't known that and I said so.

"Certainly," Williemel assured us. "We were in too much of a hurry yesterday, but going back today I'll point it out to you. That's why I know Grand Isle so well. We came here year after year. In the old days before the causeway was built it was quite a business to get here. You had to come by boat, and there was nothing but fishing camps. That's why people came. Hector Landry, he's in the Pass, he rents boats." She turned to Luz. "They catch bullreds and that's quite a sport."

Kat wanted to know instantly if they were big fish, and if so, how big.

"Fifty to sixty pounds," Williemel answered. "And then there's tarpon. Why, they have a tarpon rodeo in June and August. But all the months are good fishing except in September and February." She sighed wistfully. "This month is just perfect for fishing. But I guess you all haven't got time." She broke off, chuckling, and pointed toward the open door onto the porch. "There," she added, "look at *those* fisherman out for a catch."

We turned in time to see a flock of pelicans lumbering their way out over the surface of the Gulf, and some of us ran across the porch and to the beach to watch until, in the distance, they had settled down on the water. We walked along the water's edge and considered the possibility of a swim but decided it would be more for bravado than pleasure, because the water was not quite warm enough for more than a quick dip and the wind that still blew made the air chilly, though close to the protection of the house it was hot in the sun.

When we came back into the house Williemel was waiting with a message. Friends of hers, she said, in the oil company, learning we were there, had telephoned to ask if we would like to be flown in the company's helicopters out to their platform in the Gulf and look it over.

"He says," she amplified, "there's a pretty strong wind today and that will give us a sporty flight, but they think they can make it. I told him I'd let him know what time we'd like to go and where he could pick us up. Why, what's the matter with you, Emily?"

I suppose the blood that was freezing throughout my entire circulatory system must have given me a change of expression. It had certainly deprived me momentarily of the power of speech.

Sophy answered for me. "Williemel," she said earnestly, "Emily wouldn't even fly in the big regular plane from New York to New Orleans. She made us all come on the train. Before she'd get into a little helicopter . . ."

"I'd be dead," I managed to croak.

That took care of the helicopter excursion. Williemel went to the telephone. She would explain to her friend, she told us, that we had such a full schedule we just couldn't work it in.

"I'm not going to tell him about your feelings," she confided to me, as she left the room.

I turned on the others when she had gone and berated them for exploiting me as a craven and using that as protection. "There isn't one of you who'd get into a helicopter, especially on a gusty day like this, and you know it. Except maybe Luz."

The only answer I got was a smug smile from every one of them. And when Williemel returned, they had the gall to tell her how disappointed they were, but knowing how I felt they wouldn't want to go themselves and leave me, lest I be made unhappy about their safety.

What I could have said at that instant about my concern over their safety would have been scandalous. I went upstairs to pack.

We took a tour around the island before we returned to the mainland. The beachfront houses, we learned, were all fishing camps or cottages occupied intermittently by vacationists. The population proper lived back from the water. Williemel sat beside Clara and directed her into this back country through winding half-hidden lanes. Williemel's vocabulary for directions is one I had not encountered before. Had I been driving I could have gone astray, but Clara complimented Williemel and said for her it was much clearer than left or right.

"Turn my way," is Williemel's phrase for "To the right." "Turn your way," is her version of "Go left."

A quarter of a mile or so in from the highway we came to a settlement of little cottages that were obviously for daily living, not vacationing. Grass grew back here and trees, but the trees bore evidence of wind and storm. Their shapes were twisted. In a grove of these a clearing had been made and fenced.

"I wanted you to see this," Williemel said.

Clara stopped the car. We climbed out and as we approached the clearing saw that its fence outlined a little cemetery. All around the hidden, peaceful sanctuary the gnarled, distorted branches waved and creaked, but there was no other sound except the wind itself. We didn't talk. We moved in to read the head-stones and point out to one another with appreciation the exquisite wreaths and garlands made of delicately colored beads and encased in grass frames. One of these decorated almost every grave.

I noticed at each grave a partially burned candle, or the wax from one completely burned. I looked inquiringly at Williemel and pointed to them. The rest of the group joined us from the other car and Williemel talked with affection about this little place she had known for years, and to which we had paid our homage in that first few minutes of involuntary silence.

"Every year," she said, "a candle is placed and lighted at each grave on All Hallows' Eve. When other people are out playing Halloween pranks dressed up in fancy costume, the people here make a procession to this place, carrying candles. The candles are left here, as you see, and burn all night.

Wild ageratum and lantana grew around the graves and in such profusion they made a carpet over the whole enclosure, so thick I could not avoid stepping on bloom as I walked about to read the inscriptions. They were all in French. One inscription to a name that was certainly not French, I thought so tender I copied it down.

> Louis Chighizola
> époux d'Astaic Barthelmy
> né le 18 Fev 1820
> décédé dans le sein de la famille
> Le 24 Mars 1893

Le mort l'a fauché dans l'âge mûr
Sa chère famille eut une dépreuve trés dur
Sa vie a été sobre et industrieuse, faisant le bien
Laissant à tous un souvenir de bien
A nôtre Père!
Hier encore sur son front radieux
Nous prenions un baiser de tendresse
Hélas tu prends ton vol vers les cieux

Et tu nous laisses en pleure et en tristesse
Époux et Père adieux!

When we were back in the car I asked Williemel about the
names we had seen.

"Certainly they're not all French," she told me. "I don't know
anywhere else in the world you'd find a greater mixture in a place
of this size. You see, some of these natives are descendants of
Lafitte's pirates. This was one of Lafitte's favorite hideaways. He
got together his men and his crews from every nationality under
the sun, and a lot of them married and settled down here. There
was one, for instance, who was sort of deputy to Lafitte; they
called him Nez Coupé. He had a big oak tree in front of his house
with a hole in it. They say that's where Lafitte used to leave
messages for his deputy to get the men together." She added,
"Why, I saw you copying down what's written on his tombstone
—Louis Chighizola. That's Nez Coupé."

She pointed to a neat house we were passing. "There's a little
boy lives in that house, I expect he must be pretty nearly grown
up now. But I always used to see him when we came down here.
He's got red, tight curly hair, very thick lips, slanted eyes, only
they're bright blue, and he couldn't speak a word of any language but French."

We came back on the highway, emerging unexpectedly from
a winding lane, and I saw we were at a spot not far from the
point at which we had left it. I had marked it by the sign of
the "General Store and Post Office."

Williemel asked Clara to stop. "I'd like you all to come in and
meet Mr. Boudreaux, who owns the store. He's an old friend of
mine."

Mr. Boudreaux was pleased to meet us, he said. He was glad we
had enjoyed the island, regretted we were not to be there longer.
We promised to return. I asked if there were any places one might
stay if one were not so fortunate as to have a house. He urged
me to try the Oleander Hotel.

When we left the store I peeked into Fink's Café next door. It looked clean and pleasant. I was charting in the back of my mind a possible return someday. I would love to explore the island. I asked if we might stop for a minute at the Oleander Hotel and we did. Williemel went in with me, introduced me to the proprietor and his wife. They were old friends. And I was shown the hotel from top to bottom. It is simple and shining clean, with rooms that look out over the Gulf. It does not serve meals, but Fink's Café is close by and the owners of the Oleander told me there is a restaurant on the other side of them, too, that serves good food. I think I will go back.

Williemel said as we drove on toward the causeway that for years the only law on the island was administered by a lady judge, Judge Adams, and she administered it with a firm but fair hand. Williemel said, too, there had been another cemetery on the island. "Back on the bay," she said, "and a good many pirates were buried there. But it's gone now. The sea washed it away."

We crossed the causeway. Taking a last look back, I saw a two-wheeled cart roll onto the road we had just left. I couldn't see the face of the man who was driving the slow-moving other-world vehicle, but I thought to myself as we speeded out of sight of him, "There goes the descendant of a pirate."

Williemel was talking again. "And by the way, around here there's no Fourth of July celebration. You know why? Because that's the date of the fall of Vicksburg."

We drove past the marshes again, but this time we didn't stop to call on the Cheramies. However, to my joy, mother and daughter appeared in the doorway as we came near. Clara slowed down, we waved to them and called a *"Bonjour."* The day was sunny, the mainland was warmer than the island had been. Blue heron flew up from the marsh only a few yards from us.

I am confused about the Indians who live along that part of the Bayou Lafourche. I think they are of mixed blood and referred to as the Blues, and perhaps they are ostracized. Williemel told me about them simultaneously with the recital of her operation. I had never before been told two stories at exactly the same time and consequently my ear had not been trained to separate the themes. I know that Williemel was scared to death but didn't want anyone to know it, that she'd had her husband and son with her up to the last minute, but that she certainly had not wanted anybody else kicking around her door, on the other hand it may be the Indians who don't want that.

She also told me, veering away from Indians to Cajuns, their canoe, the pirogue, is so light and so well balanced the saying is, "It will float on a drop of dew." I had heard this before, so I know this could not refer to her operation, because in the first place she said she had put on an awful lot of weight and pretty soon was going to start taking it off, and that was why she was wearing the one dark red suit she'd started out on our trip in, because she could hardly get into anything else. So much weight made her feel downright top heavy, and she'd had her hair cut very short, too. She wasn't used to that, she didn't like the look of it and she felt off balance the way it was. None of those things could apply to a pirogue.

I saw that morning a little boy cross the bayou standing in his pirogue as I had seen his elders stand: at the stern, feet wide apart, one a little ahead of the other. He shifted his weight from the forward foot to the back, and reverse, in a slow easy rhythm, pushing the long oars from him, drawing them toward him, and the boat moved swiftly. Had the little boy been seated in the driver's seat of a car, I doubt he would have been able to see over the top of the steering wheel. I daresay he was on his way to the other side for a social call on a contemporary.

As usual, I was the first to speak of lunch. I can, however, record with accuracy that though I made a great many suggestions, this was the only one that invariably met with instant approval and co-operation. We stopped in Lockport at the Ace High Café, owned and run by Monsieur Sidney DeLaune. It was not a haphazard selection like the Huba-Huba Café. Monsieur DeLaune's establishment is one Williemel had visited many times in the past. It is famous, she said, for its turtle soup. She had held me back until we should find this particular spot, though that took two or three turns around the village of Lockport and I had chafed under such delay. I bless her for it now. She had forgotten the name of the restaurant is the Ace High Café and had been looking for a personal sign of Monsieur Sidney DeLaune.

Here is turtle soup as never I've tasted before! It is served from a big iron pot on the stove, in full view from where we sat. Monsieur DeLaune had welcomed us at the door but urged us through a front room into the one behind. We were grateful to him because there was no jukebox where we lunched. We had the room to ourselves and could sit all together at one large table looking through an open door into an immaculate kitchen and at a monumental iron pot on the stove.

A waitress served as Monsieur DeLaune dished from the pot. She set the first bowl in front of Ellen and leaning down to set it in place inquired, "Would you like your soup a little hotter?"

Ellen looked up startled and answered, "Oh no, thank you, I think I'll just take it plain."

The waitress looked at Ellen with an expression of bewildered curiosity.

Luz, sitting alongside, patted Ellen's arm soothingly and said, "She wants to know if you'd like your soup hotter."

"Oh goodness," Ellen answered, "I thought she asked if I wanted it with artichokes."

Every one of us ate more than one bowl of that thick, rich soup. I owe to Monsieur DeLaune the comforting fact that I cannot set down how many bowls we did eat. He circled the table again and again asking each time, "Wouldn't you like a little more soup put in?" But I do know that Darn ate even the cloves.

I learned, alas, that though Monsieur sells his soup canned, it cannot be shipped. This is due to some regulation he explained but I did not understand. I only know it must be purchased at his Ace High Café. I know, too, that if you buy it there you must, when serving it at home, first bring it to a boil and then add the juice of half a lemon to a quart of the soup, and in addition hard-boiled egg and sherry to taste. Monsieur DeLaune told us that with lots of eggs and hot French bread, wine and a green salad, you have a full meal. Monsieur DeLaune does not exaggerate.

We tried to buy some tins to take with us, but by the time we had finished lunch Monsieur DeLaune had gone fishing, taking with him the only key to the storeroom where his tins of soup are kept. I like having one more reason for making a return trip someday.

That afternoon we passed several rolling stores on the road. Williemel pointed out one in particular. "You see the sign on it?" she urged. And we read ELLIE DUCOS ESTATE. She explained, "That's in memory of Mr. and Mrs. Ducos. They were early settlers of this section and they got to be very prosperous with their traveling stores. Everybody respected them, the farmers, the fishermen and the trappers, and just loved them too. When they died, they were so truly mourned their descendants made the stores a kind of tombstone to them. They named them all 'Ellie Ducos Estate.' I think it's nice."

Magnolia is between Houma and Thibodaux. It is the house in which "Miss" Bessie Shaeffer lives, and we stopped to call. Miss Shaeffer was in New Orleans at the opera. The very old butler who opened the door to us explained her absence. She would be highly regretful, he assured us, to have missed Mrs. Howell and the ladies accompanying her, and she would certainly want he should show us anything we might be of a fancy to see. We stood at the doorway for a moment, looking back through a grove of magnificent magnolias, by their size very old, and for which the house is named. Among them is a sort of inner grove of beautiful live oaks hung with Spanish moss.

We walked through a wide and high-ceilinged entrance hall

and stopped at the foot of a beautiful rosewood staircase. On a gallery that runs the length of the back of the house we saw a series of slave bells of various sizes. The butler told us each was run from a different room in the house and there was no mixup in the service because the bell for each room had a different tone. The kitchen was in a separate building at some little distance, the original slave quarters beyond. Our guide showed us still another separate building constructed, he said, of double brick walls with charcoal packed between. The cistern was here, and the charcoal kept the water cool.

We were not permitted to leave until we had seen the rooms upstairs. "Miss Bessie would want you should," her representative told us sternly. They were high-ceilinged, generously proportioned, but they did not include Miss Bessie's own. Her bedroom suite was on the first floor, and as we came down the stairs, I asked Williemel if this was customary.

"Yes, it is," she said. "In a lot of the plantations you find mama and papa's bedroom and maybe a study or dressing room or whatever on the first floor, and the children's and the guests' rooms on the second."

As we walked toward the front door, preparing to go, she continued, "I want you to notice the plan of this house because I'm going to tell you about it later on, and remind me, too, to tell you a story about a gallery that goes across the front of every Southern house, or used to."

The butler saw us into our cars and, as we left the driveway, I turned back and saw him still standing at the top of the steps.

We drove about Thibodaux itself and found it a charming little town. When we left and were on the final stretch to Napoleonville, Williemel settled back and began.

"Now first of all I want to tell you about the construction of these Southern houses on the big plantations. Some of them are bigger than others, but all of them have pretty much the same plan; that's a wide downstairs hall with two big rooms on each side of it. Sometimes there are more, but it's the same number on each side, and each one of those rooms has the same number of windows in it, put in exactly the same place, and there's a reason for it. I'll tell you what it is. It's so that when you open up the front door for a breeze, there's a door just like that at the end of the hall, and you open that and the breeze goes through. And the same thing goes for the windows crosswise. You open the windows on one side, you open them on the other and the breeze runs through. That's the way you keep your houses cool as possible in this climate."

I interrupted briefly to interpolate it also provided one of the most beautiful and satisfying designs of symmetry and proportions of any type of architecture.

Williemel agreed happily. "But," she added, "it's got a terrible drawback, too. A terrible one. You're going to hear people say, or you'll read in the guidebook, 'This plantation destroyed by fire'— 'This plantation had such and such a house but it was burned.'"

"Wasn't that the awful destruction that came in the wake of what you call the War Between the States?" I asked.

"No, it was not by any means entirely that," Williemel answered quickly and vigorously. "These houses, lots of them, have burned down by themselves. Nobody set fire to them at all. It's just because of the way they're planned. Let a fire get started, and with the windows and doors exactly corresponding to each other, the flames whip through just the way a breeze does, and a house doesn't stand a chance. You can see how far out in the country they are. Time the fire department gets there from the nearest town, it's all over."

"You asked me to remind you about the galleries," I prompted her. "Have they something to do with fires, too?"

"Oh my, no," she answered. "That's a story I wanted to tell you. You know all these plantations have a downstairs gallery and most of them have an upstairs one as well. They help keep the house cool, too. Make them kind of dark, you might say. But also they're a mighty nice place to sit and get the breeze and look out at the beautiful old trees and maybe see what's going by down at the end of the driveway along the road. And that's what the story's about."

"Well," she said, "there was an editor of a small-town paper, over yonder in Mississippi. He was mayor of the town, too. And he was a well-known character all around. He ran a good paper, never afraid to say what he thought. But he had one little peculiarity. When he talked he always put in a special expression of his, and everybody who knew him knew that expression. It seems one time they had a big gathering of architects that met somewhere nearby, maybe it was in his town, I don't rightly remember. Anyway, they asked him to come and make a speech to the architects. I don't know why. He wasn't any architect, but I guess because he was the mayor and the editor. Anyway, he said he'd be delighted.

"So on the night of the speech he stamped out on the stage; the auditorium was filled. And this is what he said. 'I'm very happy to have been asked to speak to this distinguished body this evening. Indeed I am, I certainly am. And if you hadn't asked me I'd have paid you to let me come and talk to you. I would. I certainly would. It's been on my mind a long time to tell you architects what a terrible damage you are doing to the people in this part of the country. You're sending them off to mental institutions and those fellows you call psychoanalysts, you certainly are, you certainly are. And I'm going to tell you why. In the old days before you distinguished gentlemen got to monkeying with them, every house had a gallery. Most of them had two. They certainly did, they certainly did. And you know what people did on those galleries? Why, they sat in a rocking chair. And they rocked and they rocked. Lots of times when they sat down to rock they had worries, plenty of worries. They certainly did, they certainly did. But by and by as they got to rocking, they got soothed out of their worrying, that's what they did. They certainly did. Till first thing you know they were just rocking, and not worrying. They certainly were, they certainly were. And now look what's happening. You architects have come along with a lot of new ideas, everybody trying to be smarter than the next one. And what's the first thing you've done, every mother's son of you? You've taken off the galleries from our houses. You have.

You certainly have. So now we haven't got any place to rock, we let our rocking chairs go. We certainly did, we certainly did. And you know the result of that as well as I do. We got our worries but we got no rocking chairs, because we got no galleries to put the rocking chairs on and sit in and stop worrying. So instead of going to a rocking chair our people have gone to the insane asylums. They certainly have, they certainly have. And I thank you very much for allowing me the privilege of coming here this evening to tell you so. And if you hadn't invited me, I'd have paid you to let me tell you this. I would, I certainly would. I thank you very much.'"

I asked if Williemel had been at the historic meeting. She said regretfully, no, she hadn't, but immediately brightened again. "I'll tell you about the man I first heard that story from, though. I'll tell you something interesting about him. Of course everybody around here knows the story. 'They certainly do, they certainly do.' But this friend I got it from first, well, he's kind of a character, too. He's the oldest son in a big family. Has a lot of brothers and sisters and they're all married and have a lot of children, and he handles all the family's affairs. And he's a worrier. I guess maybe he needs a rocking chair. Anyway, what I was going to tell you about was this. One of the things he took on himself was the job of having a family tomb built. It was going to be big enough for all their tribe. So he got this fine monument designed, and then sure enough, he starts to worrying. You know in this part of the country, especially around New Orleans, there's always the problem of water just below the surface of the ground. You've probably seen the cemeteries around there. You know how the graves are all above ground."

I nodded. There is no opportunity for speech in one of Williemel's stories.

"Well," she said, "this man got to worrying particularly about his family tomb. Afraid it wouldn't be waterproof, and then he got himself a real crazy idea; that maybe if it was completely waterproof it would be completely soundproof, and what if somebody got buried in it and wasn't entirely dead and wanted to get out. Well, if you can believe it, he stewed and fretted over that. One day he took my husband and me out to see the tomb. And he got to carrying on about all this, and he got more and more fretful about it until I had an idea. I thought it was a fine one. I said, 'William, I tell you what to do. You get down inside your tomb and we'll close it up. And then I'll stand on it and I'll sing something for you from *Thaïs*' (because that's his favorite opera), 'and I'll sing loud for you the tune of that "Meditation" from *Thaïs*' (because that's his favorite piece), 'and then you'll find out for sure, can you hear or not.' And do you know for a fact that idea made him mad? And for the longest time after that he wouldn't speak to us. We're friends again by now, I'm thankful to say. But I never did get to sing *Thaïs* on his tomb."

A hysterical series of blasts from the station wagon's horn startled us all. Williemel stopped talking. In my absorption in her stories I had not been viewing the passing scene. As I looked now, I recognized it. We were in Napoleonville. We were on the highway.

"Turn in," I said loudly and happily to Clara and pointed to a driveway.

Mr. and Mrs. Munson had heard the horn. They were standing at the top of the steps under the porte-cochere, their arms outstretched to greet us. "Come in, come in," they were both calling as our cars stopped. "Welcome *home*."

Williemel was the first out of our car. The Munsons stared for a moment. "Williemel, Williemel," they said together, and wrapping his arms around her, Mr. Munson said to me over her shoulder, "Why, you've brought us one of our oldest friends in the world."

I wasn't surprised by this. I was beginning to take as a matter of course that everyone in Louisiana is either the oldest friend of, or kin to, very nearly everyone else.

Chapter Twelve

Sunday began with an introduction to a custom we had not heretofore encountered. Immediately we rose from the table, Mrs. Munson asked if we would join them in the sitting room for coffee. Since we had just had coffee with our breakfast, we yokels who made up the original traveling group were surprised and showed it, with one exception. Luz, our translator, our beautiful yet firm link, just like the George Washington Bridge, nodded to us reassuringly. We followed her and the others to the sitting room that was also the big downstairs hall. There we were served demitasses at half past nine in the morning. I'm sure it was out of tactful realization of our ignorance that the Munsons had not offered us this "after-dinner" coffee after our first breakfast there, but had suggested it only when there were guests for whom this was traditional. We had at least learned by now to take our coffee in cane country either unsweetened or like syrup, because if we included sugar at all, we must take "one for sweetening and one for the industry."

Williemel endeavored to make use of the opportunity this little social gathering provided to fill in some details of her operation she had previously overlooked. She was diverted from this, however, and told instead of a happy automobile accident that had occurred to her and her husband motoring through Attleboro, Massachusetts. (If there is no such place, Williemel's accent and my dullness of ear are responsible for the blunder.) Their car had been overturned, but what had made the occasion enjoyable was the discovery that the five policemen who had come to their rescue had Cajun names, although, she added regretfully, they did pronounce them with a New England accent.

Mr. Munson suggested, as we were congratulating Williemel on such a happy meeting so far from home, we might like to do a little more exploring of this neighborhood from which such people came. We accepted his suggestion at once. Emma and Clara declined. They preferred, they said, to rock awhile with Mrs. Munson and maybe a little later have another cup of coffee.

We visited first a building that is very little known outside its own community. This is the Catholic church at Paincourtville. Its interior is so delicate in color, so exquisite, the décor might have been done by Botticelli. It was, instead, done by refugee priests from Mexico. The colors are pale and translucent; they make the building itself seem not bound to earth. There are, however, practical reminders of the limitations of this planet: an electric fan and an electric alarm clock stand on the pulpit. In the wall behind the font are marble slabs with inscriptions of gratitude. *"Merci," "Actions de grâce," "De Bon Conseil, Merci."*

In the village of Paincourtville itself there are small old houses with charm, built of gray cypress and unpainted. We visited, too, the little red brick Episcopal church in Napoleonville and though this has not the beautiful murals of the other church, it has something of the same feeling of lightness because its interior is all in pale blue. The font, the altar and some of the windows have been given in memory of Mr. Munson's grandfather. Darn gathered us to see a plaque she found commemorating a citizen who had given his life at the time of the yellow fever in 1878. It didn't say how. Mr. Munson told us, as we looked, that one of the reasons it is unusual to find in the surrounding plantations much of the beautiful old furniture is that during the yellow fever plague some doctors decided perhaps the germs were contained within the houses themselves, in the hangings and the furniture. People in desperation and terror promptly emptied their dwellings, and burned the contents.

Back at Glenwood in time for lunch we found Mr. Howell. He had driven from New Orleans to gather up his "traipsin'"

Williemel. He and Mr. Munson had been boyhood friends, we learned, and at lunch we sat as spellbound as children by the reminiscences between them. Mr. Howell, tall, handsome, delightful, turned out to be as good a storyteller as Williemel. I can pay no higher tribute.

He told us, at Mr. Munson's prompting, the story of his family silver, and we secured his promise to show it to us on our return to New Orleans. The silver had come by way of a Spaniard who, having settled in Mexico, had come each winter to New Orleans for the opera season. There he had met Mr. Howell's grandparents, Mr. and Mrs. Perkins, in town for the opera, too, from their plantation. They had become friends, and Mrs. Perkins had asked the Spaniard at one time to visit at the plantation. Arriving there, he had been particularly impressed by the sheep Mr. Perkins had developed from Merino stock he had imported from Spain. This was a strain long familiar to the Spaniard, and he immediately longed to take some of it back to Mexico. A transaction had been accomplished. The Spaniard traveled with his money in trunks, the trunks filled with Mexican silver dollars. He gave six thousand of these in payment for the sheep. Mr. Perkins, in a gesture certainly as handsome as ever was, made to Mrs. Perkins a present of these silver dollars. She knew exactly to what use she wished to put them. She had heard of a famous silversmith, Italian, I think, who had migrated to Havana, Cuba. He would make her a set of fine silver from the silver she would send. The Mexican dollars were shipped to him. He melted them down and began his work. It was a task that took more than one year to accomplish, and in that interim, the War Between the States burst out. Nevertheless, the silver was shipped from Havana. It got through the blockade, was smuggled up the Bayou Lafourche and delivered to the Perkinses on their plantation. They promptly buried all of it and there it stayed untouched until the end of the war.

Williemel added a postscript to the story, "There are thirty-six pieces apart from the flatware, and I keep most of it in the original mahogany chest made by the silversmith. It's too much work to keep it polished."

The Howells and the Munsons had been neighboring plantation owners, and Mr. Munson, prompted in turn by Mr. Howell, told how the families had visited back and forth as one visited in those days, for a meal or a night, a week or a month. What fun the boys had had, fishing, shooting, trapping; and how frightened Mr. Howell had been of Mr. Munson's beautiful sisters. And then they talked of other towns and of New Orleans and cotton planters. There was a hint of condescension when that group was mentioned, perhaps because such planters lived in towns and furthermore had plantations not comparable in size with those of the sugar planters. And how compact in those days New Orleans had been; the Vieux Carré enclosing the life of the city, and itself enclosed because it had been built in such a way as to afford protection from the Indians, with Rampart Street up one side and Canal Street, the canal open then, on the other.

Mr. Howell drew us into the conversation. We must come to New Orleans at Eastertime, because Easter Day each year now marks the opening of the Fiesta. Houses and gardens in the Vieux Carré are open, and the Fiesta lasts for two weeks, and then, with a lapse of one week, is repeated. Fiesta ends with a "Night in Old New Orleans" when all the streets in the quarter are blocked off and every patio is lighted by candles.

I had seen Darn quietly open a bag in her lap, draw out notebook and pencil. Wonderful, efficient Darn. How I have blessed her for those notes, taken while I sat in contented apathy, wanting only to listen and beg the storytellers to tell more.

They did. Williemel told us about St. Martinville and the memorial park to Evangeline there. She was one of the founders and a passionate worker toward creating the Longfellow Evangeline Memorial Society. Longfellow, she said, had never visited that part of the country, but as a professor at Harvard had heard the story of Emmeline LaBiche from a student named Voorhis, and from it had written his *Evangeline*. But when she said

Emmeline LaBiche had not found her lover dying of the plague in Philadelphia, but married to another in Louisiana, and had herself gone mad from the discovery, Darn put down her pencil, saying she would make no note of that. She wanted Gabriel to die in Evangeline's arms in Philadelphia, and that was how it would be for her.

But she did write down about the vetivert grass not only because Williemel said the Longfellow Evangeline Memorial Society had wanted to plant it in the memorial park at St. Martinville in such a way as to outline the story of Evangeline, but because at the mention of the name all the other members of the Louisiana group began to tell us about the grass itself. It wasn't easy for Darn to write it down because no two members of the group proffered the same spelling when she inquired it. But they did tell us the roots of this grass dried is used by every lady in Louisiana in her linen closet and bureau drawers to scent her sheets and towels and underclothes.

Mr. Howell, because he is a lawyer, qualified the assertion; probably not *every* lady, he said. But he did agree that those who did use it had got their tradition from their foremothers and no one knew when the custom had begun.

Darn also wrote down that bunches of vetivert are sold in the souvenir shop in the memorial park in St. Martinville, and also that there is vetivert perfume as well, that can be purchased both locally and in the perfume shops of New Orleans. Clara said she thought lots of ladies changed to magnolia perfume in the summer. Darn wrote that down, too.

There was plenty of time for the stories, the information and more, while we ate lunch. To call the meal we had lunch is not only inaccurate, but an affront. We had shrimp *coquille*: tiny shrimp, mushrooms, egg, cream, sherry, covered with breadcrumbs and baked in a shell. Then turkey soup; after that broiled chicken with mushrooms, a spinach soufflé, finely cut carrot strips candied with brown sugar, lemon juice, butter and nutmeg, a stuffed prune salad and dessert of ice cream with chocolate sauce; demitasses, of course.

For two hours after this midday snack, we did nothing that required any exertion. Williemel told us more about the Cajuns. Like me, she does not count talking an exertion. At Pecan Island, she said, the citizens on Saturday night take all the furniture out of one of the houses. Not the same house; as in other communities, there is an exchange of hospitality. The guests dance all night in the empty house, and then after the women have removed their lipstick and any other makeup they may have assumed for the party, and the men have replaced the furniture, all the guests go together to mass. That concludes the party; they go home.

"Not the men, honey," Mr. Howell interrupted. "The chances are they'll go from church to the café for a game of *bourré* or euchre, and mama will send one of the kids to get him when dinner is ready, or if she needs him for something."

Clara corroborated this. "That's just what I was going to say. You wouldn't catch those Cajun men going home with their wives if there was work to be done around the house. No sir, they're going to have themselves a little pleasuring until dinner's ready."

Emma gave a contemptuous snort. She was in a rocking chair, her arms folded across her chest, and during this recital of a Cajun's weekend she had increased the tempo of its motion until now she was like a small boy on a hobby horse. "I don't know why you want to waste your time talking about those people and their carryings-on," she said. "I don't understand the way they do any more than I can understand the way they talk. When you come over west to my country, that's Lake Charles I'm talking about, I'll tell you about people that are interesting. Rice people, and oil people and politicians, everybody doing things."

"But, Emma," I broke in, "that's Cajun country too, isn't it? That's where I saw them first."

"Certainly, it's got Cajuns in it. All I say is I don't pay mind to them."

Williemel fidgeted and interrupted. "Well," she said, "if you don't all I can say is you're missing . . ."

Ellen leaned forward between them and smiled as though she were carrying an olive branch between her teeth. "Williemel," she said, "won't you tell us about your name? It's so unusual. Is it your mother's family name?"

Williemel was immediately diverted. "No, honey," she said, "it's my uncles' names. Two of them, and they were my mother's brother and my father's brother. One of them was Willie and the other was called Mel. Mama just loved them both, so she called me Williemel."

Mr. Howell did not permit the conversation to return to the Cajuns. He stood on his feet decisively and reached down a hand to Williemel. "Come on, honey," he said, "we got to be on our way if we're going to get Miss Taylor on that train. As long as she has to go, I don't want the train pulling out and us sitting along the levee in Sunday traffic."

"How far is it to New Orleans?" Luz asked.

Williemel, taking her husband's hand, let him pull her from her chair and laughed. "Don't look at me," she said, "when you ask about distance, because I never can reckon it in miles, or how long it takes you to get anywhere, because I'm always stopping along the way for something. When I was a girl I used to reckon how far it was to places by whether I could get there and home again with a beau by the time papa said I had to be in. I always remember how far Opelousas is from Lafayette because papa said we couldn't go, but we went anyway, and we got home on time. We did, we certainly did."

Mr. Howell was moving her gradually but firmly toward the door. "If we don't start right now," he said, "you're going to learn how far it is to New Orleans because we didn't get there on time."

They left and Luz went with them. We were as sorry to lose Williemel as we were to let Luz go, because in the few days she had been with us Williemel had become a friend, a gay companion, a Pied Piper guide. As I kissed her good-by, I could have wailed. "Oh, Williemel," I said, "whatever will we do without your wonderful stories?"

Behind me on the porch I heard Emma in a low voice, "I'll tell them."

We were, if anything, more reconciled to Luz's going. She had warned us she might be summoned home, and Darn, from her knowledge of calendar dates, had told us why. So we had not been bowled over when a telephone call from friends in Kentucky had reached Luz in Napoleonville saying they were coming to Little Rock for the opening of the duck season and could they stay with her. Reporting this, Luz had said of course they were right in assuming she'd be there since she hadn't missed the opening of a duck season in fifteen years.

When Luz had gone with the Howells, Mrs. Munson suggested we take a little tour with *her*. Mr. Munson had shown us places he thought we'd find interesting. She had some favorites she'd like to share.

She drove us along the Bayou Pierre Part and showed us the house of Honoré St. Germain who was called the king of Pierre Part. His royal residence has awnings. His daughter runs the Rainbow Inn close by, and Mrs. Munson told us it's a place famous for crayfish bisque. She told us, too, about the daughter. Her father had sent her to be educated in a fashionable convent in New Orleans. She had gone obediently, had been a good student, completed her education with high standing, and had then announced to her father the only thing she wanted to do was to come back and live in the swamps by the bayou she loved. Her father bought the Rainbow Inn and set her up as proprietor.

We watched a man rowing his family in a pirogue across the Bayou Pierre Part. Mrs. Munson told us there is no road on the far side; their only outlet to other communities is by pirogues. There are many communities like that, she said, and a common expression among their inhabitants is, "Haven't been out front lately." That means they haven't been as far as the highway along the Bayou Lafourche.

We came to Belle River. Mrs. Munson pointed across it to a levee and told us that twenty miles beyond is another levee, and between the two the Atchafalaya Spillway runs north and south for two hundred miles protecting the countryside now from the floods that had brought disaster to the Munsons and all their neighbor planters. This is where, Mrs. Munson also told us, the famous Belle River big blue crabs are found.

We drove on a rough but passable dirt road along the bayou. Mrs. Munson said she was hoping to find there would be a *fais do do* that evening. But when we stopped to ask about it from a group of men in front of a café, we were told there would be no *fais do do* because of the grinding. It was strange to see a "café" so labeled in this far-off little settlement. But when I told Mrs. Munson it seemed strange to me, she assured me however remote and small the settlement, there would always be found a place in which to hold a *fais do do* and games of *bourré*.

We passed a small lumber yard stacked with cypress, and there we had trouble with Ellen. Delighted with the beauty of the wood, Ellen declared it exactly what she and Lloyd wanted for the terrace of their new house in Bedford, and if we could find the man who ran the lumber yard, she would talk to him about shipping what she would need. Then she would go back to the Munsons' and try to reach both her husband and the architect by telephone; if they could give her the measurements and the amount required, she would return and place her order.

Kat was appalled at the suggestion. She pointed out a few of the difficulties to be surmounted in accomplishing this transaction and flouted the whole idea as wildly impractical. Sophy explained to Kat that for Ellen if an idea was appealing, its practical accomplishment was irrelevant, and certainly only a minor detail.

Ellen paid attention neither to Kat nor to Sophy. She asked Mrs. Munson to stop the car, got out, wrote down the name of the place, explored it, but found no one in its vicinity and returned to the car. She would put in the telephone calls, she told us, and then try to return. If there was not time for this, she would write back when she got home.

"It ought to be an interesting correspondence," was Darn's comment.

"Well, after all, dear," Ellen answered, "I can write French. I only need to explain how I happened to see his beautiful lumber and then tell him about our house and what we need."

We drove on.

A little girl came running along the road toward us. She had on a crisply starched pink dress. Her ears were pierced and she wore tiny gold hoop earrings. She was calling, *"Maman, maman."* A pretty young woman came from a cabin, walked to the fence that separated it from the road and waved to the little girl. We stopped the car and talked to both of them. The mother spoke no English. The child was her daughter, seven years old, and went to school. Her name was Félice. We asked if she spoke English and Félice answered in English that she did, and was teaching Maman and Papa.

"You see," Mrs. Munson said as we left them, "this is what compulsory education is doing. The children are teaching the parents to speak English."

We stopped again to watch a family arrive by pirogue at a houseboat drawn up along the bank. The husband, tall, handsome, carried a little boy about two years old. The wife, tall, too, dark and pretty, carried in her arms a baby. The husband was shy and went immediately into the houseboat. The little boy came running out a minute later; the mother grabbed him as he toddled past and held tightly to his hand. She laughed and explained in French he was not used to a houseboat and would walk right off it into the water, so she must be careful all the time when they came to visit grandmamma. She spoke no English and explained the houseboat belonged to her mother, who lived alone on it. Her father was dead. But every Sunday she, her husband and the two children came from across the bayou where they lived for supper. The baby was only six months old. She was safe, but they would tie a long rope to the little boy and attach it to something far enough away from the rail of the porch, or deck, so he could not fall in.

On our way back to Napoleonville, I asked Mrs. Munson to tell us about Glenwood Plantation in the old days.

She thought for a minute or two before she spoke and I knew she was living rapidly back over the years. "It was all new to me," she began, "when I came here as a bride. I grew up in New Orleans. I was a city child. I knew very little about plantation life but I loved it from the very start.

"We all lived together in the big house: my husband's brothers and their wives. Their father was dead and they ran the plantation. There weren't any highways then, I can tell you. There was only a mile and a half even of gravel road; the others were just plain mud, I called them. But Edward always used to correct me. They were soil, he said. The boys worked hard. They'd be out in the fields before daybreak and then, about seven o'clock, we girls would ride on our horses out to where they were working, and the servants would come along driving a buggy or a cart, with breakfast in it. They'd set up a table right by the field where the men were, and we'd all sit around and have a big, hot breakfast. The men would rest a little while after that and then they'd go back to work; the servants would pack up the things, and we girls would go for a ride and then back home, where there was plenty for each of us to do with the running of a big plantation.

"Then there were parties, of course, up and down the bayou at all the plantations. And we went back and forth to New Orleans in the winter after the grinding. And in the spring everybody from the plantations would get together in whatever town they were holding a sale of mules; in those days all the hauling in the fields was done by mules. We didn't have trucks, and they even used mules for some of the grinding; they didn't have the kind of machinery they have now. You paid almost as much for a good mule as you do today for a car. Fifteen hundred dollars wasn't unusual. They were shipped in mostly from Kentucky and lots of them came from around St. Louis, and wherever the sale was, all the plantation owners would gather. We'd have a high old time. The sales lasted for several days. We'd have dances and picnics and all kinds of carryings-on. Plenty of servants; I don't really know how many people worked on the place.

"Of course they didn't have the schools then like they do now, that compulsory education we were talking about a little while ago, and you saw what it's doing. When my husband was growing up there was a tutor in every plantation for the boys, and a governess for the girls. Then when the boys got old enough they were sent, mostly up North to a university, lots of times to England; Cambridge, Oxford. Girls went abroad, too, to finish their education. Everybody traveled a lot in those days." She smiled and added, "In spite of the mud roads and slow boats. Nowadays people have highways. But people like us don't get a chance to use them much. The depression and the big floods," she broke off a minute and laughed a low quiet laugh from inner amusement, "well, they washed out our traveling. I guess you might say we were washed up."

We turned in the driveway of Glenwood and stopped under the porte-cochere. Mr. Munson came out to meet us.

"Edward," Mrs. Munson said, "entertain these ladies for a little while, will you please? Supper's going to be a little bit late. I have to see to it and I hadn't meant to be out so long."

For supper we ate *boudin*. That, we learned, is a dish made of pork with rice and herb seasoning; head cheese; potato salad; cold ham and a lemon pie. Mrs. Munson came from the kitchen to tell us it was ready. But after dinner she sat in the drawing room and served us *café brûlot*.

Chapter Thirteen

IF I SHOULD HAVE TO ISOLATE FROM THE WHOLE TRIP ONE expedition that stood out from all the rest, fascinating as they were, I would name the voyage of Monday, November 15, on the U.S. Mail Boat 20W514; more informally named *The Addie*.

We were up at half past five. Darn, of course, was the one who wakened us. Sophy, Ellen, Darn and I were the only ones going on this tour. Kat had decided to stay at home. Whatever came of it, she said, a trip that began at five-thirty in the morning was not to her liking, but a day of rest and rocking with Emma and Clara appealed to her. It had been Ellen's idea, then, to move into Darn's room for the night, so that Kat would not be disturbed by the early riser. Kat had applauded this suggestion so enthusiastically she had helped Ellen transfer her equipment for the trip.

We dressed in slacks and sweaters; it was cold at that early hour. We took raincoats, and scarves to tie over our hair; Sophy and I each carried a camera and an extra sweater. We came from our room at the moment Ellen and Darn tiptoed into the hall. Even in the darkness I could see they carried considerable equipment, too, and something that stood out lighter than the rest indicated Darn was wearing white gloves.

We tiptoed down the stairs, saw no one in the dining room but heard sounds beyond it, and, exploring, found the kitchen and Mr. and Mrs. Munson there, getting breakfast. Mrs. Munson reluctantly allowed us to help, only because this enabled her to make sandwiches to add to our other equipment. She told us we must also take a thermos of coffee and one of water, and she would have these ready, too. We ate a great deal, protesting as usual we never, never ate such a hearty breakfast. By six-thirty we were ready to leave. We climbed into Mr. Munson's car with some little difficulty of placement because of the extras each of us was carrying.

At twenty minutes to seven we were parked in front of the post office in Napoleonville and, in spite of sweater and leather jacket, I was chilly. Mr. Munson insisted I let him try to get home and back with a windbreaker jacket for me. He could make it, he was sure, before the postman arrived. If not, we could go on without it. We got out of the car and he drove off. We stood on the pavement outside the post office and put in a heap at our feet all the things we had been carrying. We watched the druggist come to his shop across the street. He waved to us as he unlocked the door. Through the store windows we saw him turn out the night light in the back room, take some jars off a shelf, setting them on a high counter in front of him. I suppose he was going to make up a prescription, but I was diverted by a conversation in French on the corner opposite to us between a woman and a little boy carrying papers. She was demanding he take one of his morning papers to the ladies in front of the post office. And he, in turn, refused because, he said, it was not on his route, and furthermore, it would make him one paper short for his delivery. If she wished to take us one from the pile he was leaving for her newsstand, *bien sûr*, that was the thing to do. He rode off on his bicycle.

The woman brought a paper across to us. She had on a black sweater over a cotton dress and had pulled the sweater tight, wrapping it beyond the buttons and holding it across her front with one arm. It was cold, she said; probably it would rain a little. We talked about the independence of young people nowadays and what ought to be done about it.

Mr. Munson's car came around the corner so fast its tires protested. He stopped it at the spot from which he had taken off.

At the moment he got out waving a jacket toward me, another car pulled in behind, and its driver, leaning out the window, waved his arm and a cigar he was holding and called out, *"Bonjour . . ."*

It was an old car. When the driver getting out slammed the door, the whole structure suffered a momentary palsy. Mr. Munson shook hands with the new arrival and introduced him to each of us. Mr. Oufnac.

Mr. Oufnac was dismayed to find there were four of us. We would not be entirely comfortable, he said in French and English, and further it would require his procuring an extra life preserver. Would one of us, perhaps, like to stay behind?

We told him emphatically one of us would not. We assured him we did not have to be comfortable. We coaxed him to find, without too much trouble, another life preserver, if that was required. Happily, he was persuaded.

He told us to enter the car. He would join us shortly when he had secured the mail.

I put on Mr. Munson's jacket, and when this was added to the padding I already wore, I had considerably less than freedom of movement. Nevertheless, I managed to pull myself into the old vehicle, and was in the front seat when Mr. Oufnac returned from the post office dragging two large sacks of mail. He stowed these away in the luggage compartment, returned to the driver's seat, slammed the door after him, and this enabled us all to participate in the resultant tremor. With hideous noise he put the poor old thing in gear, leaned out his window with another flourish of his cigar toward Mr. Munson. The rest of us waved, too. With a lurch we bounded from the post office. Mr. Munson called, "Take care."

As soon as we had left the village limits and were on a winding dirt road, Mr. Oufnac steered his ancient over to the extreme left lane and held it there. In the next ten miles, without slackening speed, he lit his cigar seven times. This is by Darn's count, so it is accurate. He didn't talk much at first. This may have been because none of us found anything to say to him. If the others

were in the panic I was experiencing, and only a senseless clod
would not have been panicked, they were like me physically
unable to speak.

Our king of the road presently turned off on a cart track, little
more, that was rocky but ran through beautiful woods. Two miles
on this brought us to a clearing and a cabin. Its owner, hearing
us coming—and even a dull ear would have caught the sound—
came out to meet us. He was a large man, tall, heavy but not fat,
with broad shoulders and a straight vigorous carriage. He was
Mr. Ernest Aucoin, we learned, as we leaned out and shook
hands all around. He spoke only French but his speech was clear
and precise, easy to understand. Mr. Oufnac had put two letters
on a seat between us. He must have removed them before he
had stacked the sacks at the post office. He gave these to Mr.
Aucoin, who glanced at the envelopes with a clear-sightedness
that did not require holding them very close to his eyes, nor very
far away. I saw, as it changed hands, one of these two pieces
of mail was from Father Flanagan's Boys Town. I know very
little about the way mailing lists are assembled, but it must be
a remarkable system that can draw in Mr. Aucoin. I wondered
what address Mr. Aucoin uses, but I didn't like to ask.

We returned, of course, the way we had come, and once we
were on our original back road again, hugging its left side, we
talked. My sensation of panic had spread out to a kind of over-
all numbness that at least restored my physical ability to speak.
Evidently the others went through the same transformation because we all talked. In answer to our questions, Mr. Oufnac told
us he makes his delivery trip on Mondays, Tuesdays, Wednesdays
and Fridays, and that he has been doing it for twenty-one years.
He is delighted to take passengers and charges $5 per person for
the day's trip.

I asked where we were and was told the road, on which
we were facing instant death around every bend, is called the
Atakapas. I was sorry I'd asked. I had to get him to spell it three
times before I could get it written down. This made him impatient.

I asked where he lived and he said at Belle River (that was easier). He told us about the flood in 1927 when the levee broke at Torrance. It brought seven feet of water, he said, where he lived, and the whole cane crop round about was lost. It had been ruined the year before, he added, by a heavy freeze. And those two years were what had put most of the plantations out of business and into "the hands of the bank." But now, he went on to say, the Spillway has changed all that. He even smiled, and I saw a dreamy look come over his face before he spoke again, to tell us they were building a road on the Spillway levee and in a few weeks it would be shell all the way to Morgan City. A wonderful thing. He'd been courting in Morgan City for eighteen years, a woman of sixty-five now, but hadn't made up his mind as yet to get married. However, the shell road would probably make a lot of difference.

We passed a small pond and Mr. Oufnac waved his cigar toward it. "Belongs to a friend of mine," he said. "Made it himself and he does fine business by it."

"What does he do with it?" I asked, and wished to God I hadn't spoken, because Mr. Oufnac turned a full right angle to look at me with astonishment and something of contempt.

"*Alors,* he keep it full of turtles. Supply restaurants with turtles all the way up to the big city."

It is impossible to reproduce the criss-crossing of French and English Mr. Oufnac spoke, and at that moment I hoped he would say nothing more in any language, but only look to his driving, such as it was.

We didn't speak again because we had come to the end of our drive. He whirled us around one more bend and mercifully nothing was coming toward us at the end of the turn. He reversed the wheel, we careened over to the right side of the road, he plunged his foot down on the brake, the ancient vehicle shuddered, stopped. We had arrived.

We were alongside a bayou, narrow and choked with water hyacinths. Drawn up at the bank was a boat that would be difficult to list under any specific category.

We got out of the car, walked over to the bank and looked down at this conveyance that was now to be ours. The center part was roofed over, and windows ran along the side of this center structure. We saw a seat across the back covered with leather that had cracked with age, and in front of this, in the very center of the boat, an ancient gasoline engine in an open pit. Behind the main house, so to speak, was a stubby stern, and ahead an uncovered but fairly long bow. But this was no outcast among boats, no tramp ship! This was a government carrier. It said so in large black letters along the side: US MAIL BOAT, 20W514; and a little farther on toward the bow Mr. Oufnac's own name for it, *The Addie*. A salute, I daresay, though I didn't ask, to the lady in Morgan City.

Our chauffeur, now become captain, bustled about, transferring his sacks of mail to *The Addie* and with some grumbling searching in sheds nearby for an extra life preserver. If it were anything but a government boat he wouldn't bother with it, he assured us, but as a government official he must observe the law. No part of his scruples, we understood clearly, was directed toward our personal safety.

An old man was bailing out a boat tied alongside *The Addie* and we talked to him. He was not in good humor and he told us why. He had rented out his boat to a pair of foreigners for duck hunting. They'd got some fine mallards and canvasbacks, but they had returned his boat dirty. He muttered in a guttural French his opinion of such people. I couldn't catch the words but the sentiment was not difficult to translate.

Mr. Oufnac returned, a life preserver over his arm, and told us we could go aboard. We crawled through a narrow opening, down into the middle section. Three of us squeezed into the seat in the stern, the fourth, Sophy, wedged herself into a corner beside us on a narrow bench. Captain Oufnac settled himself on a straight-backed chair in the very center, facing his engine. He lighted a fresh cigar, bent over the motor, and turned things with both hands. Suddenly the engine roared, the boat shook, and we were ready to go. The captain cast off, steered away from the bank, and we moved slowly down the bayou, waving out the back window to the old man standing in his boat. He stopped long enough to give us an answering wave.

For a few minutes Captain Oufnac was not happy, nor were we when we felt and saw water sloshing about our feet. He took up a lard tin from the floor beside his chair and bailed a little. Then, turning around to us, he said we must distribute ourselves differently. We had brought the boat too low in the water. We were ready and eager to co-operate. We tried various adjustments and combinations, and eventually settled on a distribution that put Ellen and Sophy standing on the stubby stern, resting their elbows on and balancing themselves against the roof of the center part. Darn and I, bent double, eased our way along the length of the boat, squeezed past the captain, and climbed through a window to sit in the bow, our backs braced against the center structure, our feet straight out ahead. We were happy to be there. Inside I had felt a little squeamish from the heat of the engine and the smell of gasoline mixed with the captain's cigar.

I never saw a man have such difficulty keeping a cigar alight. I've associated such endeavor with a pipe smoker; but all the time Captain Oufnac worked over his engine, he constantly relit his cigar. I mentioned to Darn I thought we would probably blow up at any moment. Her comforting answer was she had entertained the same supposition but had dismissed it with the realization that Captain Oufnac had told us he had been making this trip in exactly this fashion for twenty-one years. From the looks of it this must be the same boat he had used during that entire period, and therefore there was no more likelihood of its blowing to bits on this one than of all those Mondays. I found this reasoning sound and allowed the cigar and the matches to give me no further anxiety.

Turning a little I could see back through the window through which we had crawled, and I watched with interest the captain arrange his business. Except for Mr. Landry's rolling store I have never seen a small area so densely stocked and with such variety: oddments of tools, boxes of cigars, food supplies of a range certainly to supply an extremely catholic taste; fishing rods, oilskins, sweaters and a great deal of what could only be listed as miscellaneous.

Running along the side at the captain's right and within easy reach were seventeen open boxes in a double row. When the captain had us properly assorted and the engine running to his satisfaction, he opened his sacks of mail and, with remarkable dexterity, sorted *it*, putting pieces into the several boxes, and at the same time steering *The Addie*.

We chugged out into open water and called back to ask the captain its name.

"Lake Verret," he shouted back to us over the snorting of the engine, and pointed as we passed it to a large kerosene lamp that swung from a pole. It was lighted at night, he explained, to mark the entrance to the bayou. We would see such markings frequently, he told us.

"Like street signs," I said.

"*C'est ça*," he answered.

Darn whispered to me, "He's in wonderful humor now."

I nodded agreement. He had come into his own domain. He was the captain of his ship, this was the world he knew and enjoyed, and he expanded with pleasure at having visitors aboard to whom he could show and explain it.

The day was turning out to be gray and overcast and we were thankful for it. Since we had had to be distributed outside, we counted it the best of fortune that the hot sun was not blazing down on us, unprotected as we were. Silver fish were jumping hysterically on all parts of the lake, dotting its surface with silver exclamation points. There was no traffic other than the passage of our own boat; its engine created the only noise to be heard, except for a sound like rain when big drops fall, that the fish made, leaping out and dropping back into the water.

We had left the water hyacinths in the bayou. I asked the captain why there were none in the lake. He told me to look back where the kerosene lamp hung; I could perhaps see a wire stretched across the mouth of the bayou. Anyway, it was there to keep the water hyacinths from spreading into the lake.

Darn, who is a knowledgeable and always inquiring gardener, asked if the hyacinths were indigenous. She had to amplify and explain that, but the captain, once he understood, told her he'd heard they'd been brought from Japan originally and just took over. I told Darn Mrs. Munson had given me an explanation when I had asked the same thing, though I am no gardener, and I preferred hers.

There was an Indian girl, a legend says, whose lover went away promising to return. She waited for him sitting on the bank of a bayou, where she had waved him out of sight as he paddled toward the big water. He never came back, or if he did, she was not there to greet him. She had fallen into the water and where she had disappeared water hyacinth bloomed.

Darn said she found this explanation unsatisfactory.

At the far side of the lake we entered another bayou, and from that moment until hours later, when we recrossed the lake returning home, I had not the faintest notion of where we were in relation to where we had been half an hour earlier. But my respect for our captain mounted so that it completely erased (that is until our journey back to Napoleonville) my distrust of him as a chauffeur. How a man sorting mail, keeping in operation an old and troubled engine, and overcoming his own personal difficulty in keeping a cigar lighted, could navigate through and around those labyrinthian tortuous bayous, knowing not only where he was but where he was going. I do not know. I have an urge, however, to write Admiral Byrd that here is a man, Captain Oufnac, indispensable to any expedition into the unknown.

For the first time since we had cast off we saw an area where people lived: three or four little cabins in a clearing and a rude landing dock. At the moment I caught sight of them I very nearly fell off the bow into the bayou because a raucous earsplitting blare sounded off immediately behind me. When I had caught my balance and clutched Darn, who appeared to be sliding down the side away from me, I turned and so did she, to see what on earth had happened inside. The captain, enthusiastically blowing his cigar into a violent torch, was pulling on a cord suspended above him from bow to stern like the line a conductor used to pull on an old-fashioned trolley to mark up his fares. This line, and I had not noticed it before, when pulled, blew a horn: And the captain was pulling it to beat the band.

They heard it in the cabins. How could they not? Two or three people came out, among them an old lady who was wearing a bright-colored cotton dress and a sunbonnet, though the day was overcast. We nosed in alongside the dock; the old lady squatted on her haunches. Oufnac reached up and out his window to hand her a bundle of mail. She was evidently the post-mistress because she immediately re-sorted the mail in her hands and doled it out to others who had followed her. While she was doing this she held an animated conversation with our captain, stooping down to catch his answers to her questions, and rising again to hand out a letter to one of her companions. The conversation was entirely in French and very rapid, but I gathered she had placed an order for stamps. The captain delivered these and she reached into a pocket of her dress, pulling out a worn leather purse, like a pouch, with a chased silver clasp. My great-grandmother had one like that. The captain at the request of the postmistress also wrote down a request for some money order blanks that he would bring on his next trip. They finished their business and we backed nosily from the dock and headed up the bayou again.

During the next hour or so we saw neither people nor houses. We moved between giant cypresses hung with Spanish moss that fringed either bank; palmettos grew beneath, and as far as we could see on either side was black swampland, heavily wooded like jungle growth. We watched blue heron and white egrets fly up from the water startled by the sound of our approach. We saw others roosting awkwardly on cypress branches.

In this bayou the water hyacinths grew thick and at the end

of half an hour or so we came upon cows standing in the water apparently grazing on them. Farther on was another dock. A woman in a sunbonnet sat on it, fishing. We drew up beside her and saw she was barefooted. She had caught seventeen perch; Darn counted them. We had some conversation with her while the captain gathered together the mail for this point of delivery. A man came out of a cabin set back from the dock. The woman made no motion to collect the mail. The man was evidently the one in authority here. He talked with us a little when he had taken letters from the captain, and noticing a watch on Darn's wrist asked if we would mind waiting while he went back to his cabin and got his alarm clock. He would like to set it. The captain assured him we would wait because he had some packages for delivery here and needed a little extra time to write out the receipts to be signed for them. The alarm clock was set, the packages delivered—those I could see came from Sears, Roebuck—and we headed up the bayou again.

At our next stop about an hour later, Captain Oufnac suggested we might like to leave the boat for a few minutes since he was going to refuel. It was a delicate suggestion and we took advantage of it.

A dozen or so cabins made up this little community, larger than the other two stopping places. We walked behind the row that fringed the bayou and found a second row behind and in between a considerable open area like a village green, and beyond that, to our astonishment, rising a considerable height, a levee, with men working along the top it. Evidently this was the road being laid with shell to Morgan City. I would have thought we were many miles away from any road whatsoever. There were children playing on the village green, a young woman was hanging wash on a line to dry, three or four men were standing outside a nearby cabin that looked as if it might perhaps be a general store. We saw a new cabin in construction. As we approached it, two workmen came from it, passed us, asking if we were from the mail boat. We went behind the cabin and found, as we had hoped, a brand-new outhouse. Ellen was the first to

take advantage of this discovery. The rest of us waited, watching life on the green. When she returned, she brought us news of it, but as Sophy pointed out, this seemed a curious time and place for Ellen to choose to use the French language to convey privately to us we need not be in the least afraid, the place was very clean and neat, altogether nice. It was the one place, as Sophy emphatically told Ellen, in which French was the only language understood by the people around us. All Ellen needed to do to insure such personal comments not being shared was to speak in her native English.

When we returned to *The Addie* the refueling was not quite completed, and the audience had grown. Besides the workmen from the new cottage, the children from the green, and their mothers, one or two citizens had strolled down for the big event of the mail delivery. The postmaster was pleased. He was holding an airmail letter in his hand and showed it to us. It was from one of his sons, he said, still in the service. He had five, and all had served their country; the youngest was just back from Korea. He showed us the letter and I read the address: "Via Napoleonville, Marine Route Number One."

Just as we were pulling out a pretty young woman came running along the dock. She was blonde and had a bunch of flowers pinned at the neck of her blouse. She waved a package and Oufnac nosed the boat back to the dock to receive it. It was to her husband in Germany, she explained, and we were all glad it had not missed the boat.

We ate our sandwiches out on the bow. Ellen and Sophy joined Darn and me there and when we had eaten Darn and I changed places with them. But as we left we warned them not to expect too great comfort from the change. It might be tiring to stand in the stern, I said, but they would find it excruciating to sit with legs stretched out in front of them and no change of position possible; a pillow should be on the list of passenger equipment. Nevertheless, I added quickly, muscular agony or not, I would not have taken anything for this day, nor would

I ever forget it. No one contradicted me. I like, too, to remember such rare moments.

At half past four we tied up at our own landing. We had traveled eighty miles in *The Addie* the captain told us and added, with the pride of a successful businessman, we had taken $225 in money orders. He followed the left side of the road all the way back to Napoleonville. We were not killed. We were tired, hungry, but happy; not too tired to eat a dinner of green pea soup, oysters farcis, steak, creamed potatoes and dewberry cobbler, but tired enough to go to bed immediately after the *café brûlot.*

I went to sleep with the sound in my ears of water lapping, the sharp clap of a crane's wing taking off in flight, and matches striking as Captain Oufnac lighted his cigar.

Chapter Fourteen

THE MUNSONS SENT US ON OUR WAY TUESDAY WITH A
last Cajun story at breakfast. Mr. Munson said a few years ago
their son, who is married now and a father, was sitting talking
to a Cajun girl at a high-school dance in Napoleonville when
a young Cajun boy came up and spoke to her.

"Are you engaged?" he began.

The girl answered, "I was never met with you before."

The boy's reply to that was, "Oh, don't be such a children,"
and with that held out his hand. She took it obediently and they
walked off together leaving the Munsons' son disconcerted, but
no match for a Cajun in the matter of handling a situation in-
volving a girl.

All morning we drove through cane country; men in the fields
to either side of us were swinging horrifying-looking tools that
looked like giant cleavers. Whatever their name, the purpose of
these was unmistakable. The fields were being cleaned up to
make ready for the next crop since this one had been cut and
carted to the grinding mill. We didn't stop to talk to the workers,
in fact we paid no calls on any residents and made no stops until
we reached Morgan City, and that was a record for the trip because Morgan City is almost two hours from Napoleonville.

In Morgan City we called on the editor of the newspaper,
with whom we had a delightful conversation though he was a
little irked that we were only passing through. We were even
more rueful about this than he, I assured him, but friends were
waiting for us at New Iberia and we were scheduled to spend

the night on Avery Island. "That," I said, "is the difficulty of a schedule. Once you've made it, you have to keep it. Next time I'll throw a schedule out the window and just drift from bayou to bayou."

We were taken to the Twin City Fisherman Co-op. Fifty shrimp boats operate through this organization, but we did not see the boats themselves because the fleet was out. We saw, however, the beheading tables, the conveyors a little more elaborate than the ones at Grand Isle, but on the same principle, flowing with ice water to keep the shrimp cold and to get the slime off. We learned that workers are paid one cent a pound for beheading, and that in a week of big catch they average forty to fifty dollars. The workers come running when the siren blows to tell them the fleet is coming in. I hope the handbell at Grand Isle is never replaced by a siren.

I had not known until our guide told us that Morgan City is the big port for the fur industry and for shells. Like the bell-man in "The Hunting of the Snark," I've said it once, I've said it twice, what I say three times is true. And what I say is I am an ignorant woman, and that is true, and furthermore, my awareness of this increases with every trip I take.

The matter of shells for instance. Shells, in my span of knowledge were delicate, exquisite objects to be picked up and enjoyed on a stroll along a beach. That is not what happens to shells in Morgan City. They are crushed and shipped for such purposes as roads on which we had traveled, cement, animal mashes, poultry feed, and the manufacture of lime. I never would have thought of such a thing.

We drove to Morgan City's twin city, that is Berwick, over the bridge that spans the Atchafalaya River, and as we crossed it Clara told us the standard test for a citizen of Louisiana is that he must have lived in the State long enough to know how to spell the Atchafalaya River, the street in New Orleans called Tchoupitoulas, and the town of Natchitoches.

We didn't stop in Berwick nor farther on at Franklin, nor Jeanerette. Franklin had beautiful old houses and Darn read from the guidebook that the settlement had been founded in 1800 by a Pennsylvanian who had named it in honor of his hero, Benjamin Franklin, but that French and Spanish families were included among its first citizens.

Emma knew and told us about the occupants of nearly every one of the beautiful houses. She would have liked us to pay calls, but we rushed on, through Jeanerette, where we saw sugar mills and the roads outside crowded with cradle trucks brimming over with cane waiting to be ground. And in every village and town we passed, the main street was lined with oaks, and these were hung with moss.

We were in New Iberia for lunch, just as Sophy had planned. It was closer to a two o'clock than twelve o'clock lunch, but at least she had said we would eat in New Iberia and we did. She had mentioned this a number of times. We ate gloriously at the Frederick Hotel. Naturally, its proprietor was a friend of Emma's and they had a happy reunion. The proprietor is Mrs. Southwell and the hotel is an exclusively family business. Mrs. Southwell was formerly Mrs. Patout. She and her husband, before his death, administered their property with personal supervision of every department. They sent their two sons, Jean and Gerald, to what Mrs. Southwell called a "hotel college." The young men are graduates now of the college, but not of mama. She still administers from the front office. Jean and Gerald, in white coats, have charge of the kitchen and dining room. We ate the best crayfish bisque we had anywhere on the trip, and with it a green salad with Roquefort dressing, garlic bread toasted—I eschewed with a shudder that the very mention of garlic sends over me (but there were plain toasted rolls for me)—chocolate French cake and ice cream, at which my figure ought to shudder.

Mother and sons urged us to be their guests at dinner on the following night, when they would prepare for us a meal to include both venison and wild duck. But that, too, had to be put off for another trip because of the wretched schedule. I unabashedly placed the blame for our omissions and deprivations on Sophy, because she had made the schedule. Sophy protested hers was certainly a thankless job. Far from appreciation for the work she had done with maps, all she got was abuse. But when I asked if she would like to resign her position as executive director, she said flatly she would not consider such a thing, and there was no further discussion.

We were not expected at Avery Island until late afternoon, and so after lunch we had time to drive to St. Martinville. We visited the Catholic church there and the cemetery behind, with its statue of Evangeline. Just beyond the church Emma pointed out a little bakery that is widely famous for its rusks and French bread. We considered visiting it, not that even I after such a lunch could nibble anything more, but Kat thought we might lay by an investment against future hunger pangs. Ellen pointed out convincingly that since we were spending the night as guests of the McIlhennys' it would not be altogether polite for us to arrive carrying a loaf of French bread because its length would be difficult to conceal about one's person. Reluctantly we passed by the bakery with stopping. By mutual agreement we did not endeavor to find coush-coush recommended by Mr. Joseph.

But we did make purchases in the little handicraft shop that is just within the gates of the Evangeline Memorial Park, bunches of vetivert root for our linen shelves and hand-woven guest towels made in that region. The custodian of the shop, a vivacious lady, addressed us each as *"Chère"* and prefaced every sentence by this appellation. She had interesting things to tell us: That the shop is itself a fine example of Acadian architecture. It is a story-and-a-half building with a flight of steps that runs from the edge of the covered front porch directly beside the front door to the space enclosed under the slanting roof above. That the Acadians, descendants of the original settlers in 1775, have consistently maintained their weaving, their crafts and their way of life. That for many years these bayou people of the Teche country have been isolated from the rest of Louisiana, and only comparatively recently gained a knowledge of the outside world by virtue of field work done by the Louisiana State University.

I examined rugs and bedspreads wistfully, but was dissuaded

from purchasing them by Sophy who said if I added such bulk to what we were already carrying, I could thumb my way back to New Orleans.

We returned Emma and Clara to the Frederick Hotel with the agreement to rejoin them the following day after lunch. When we left, Emma was rocking in Mrs. Southwell's front office.

We saw Avery Island long before we reached it. It rises astonishingly above the surrounding flat landscape, and by contrast to the marshes is startlingly green and wooded. The island is owned by the McIlhenny and Avery families and the McIlhennys are relatives of Kat's husband. We were indebted to Kat for our invitation to spend the night as their guests. Kat reminded us of this when we reached the McIlhenny property, with a special observation to Sophy that from now on she would take charge.

Sophy acquiesced so submissively Kat was alarmed and urged her not to behave in an unnatural fashion.

Our new leader coached us in the pronunciation of the name McIlhenny, with "h" silent, and extracted our promise not to forget it. She told us something about the island itself, in spite of Darn's reminder that it was all in the guidebook.

The Averys and the McIlhennys, who are related, have owned and lived on the island for a number of generations, but it was Mr. Edward Avery McIlhenny who made it a place travelers must visit. He died a few years ago, but during his lifetime he created and developed the bird sanctuary and the gardens, accomplishments that seem almost impossible of achievement during one man's span of years. Instead of using his knowledge of ornithology and horticulture as a basis for further research, he shared it with anyone who cares to come and see.

The bird sanctuary began as a haven for egrets. In the 1890's Mr. McIlhenny had found this exquisite bird was almost extinct. He explored the swamps until at last he and two Negro assistants found seven young birds. He brought them home and in 1893 had a small colony for which he established the sanctuary.

We were on the island now and stopped at a toll gate, but when Kat gave her name, the gatekeeper told her we were expected and were not to pay the tourists' admission fee of fifty cents per person, plus a dollar a car. Kat accepted this news as a personal triumph. The gatekeeper gave us directions for finding the Tabasco factory. He said Mr. McIlhenny was waiting for us there.

There are "any God's quantity" of roads, as Sophy put it, on the island, and not one seems to be any more "main" than another. I made the mistake of expressing aloud my thankfulness we'd been given directions. I ought to have known by now that Sophy's dislike of being told where to go is only aggravated by my being grateful for it.

"I could have done better with a map," she said tartly.

Ellen, the dove, immediately asked Kat about the Tabasco factory the gatekeeper had mentioned, and Kat, delighted to give further information, told us that all the Tabasco sauce in the world is made on Avery Island by the McIlhenny Company. It takes its name from the town Tabasco, Mexico, where the pepper seeds were found. They were brought back by a United States soldier returning from the Mexican War. He had given the seeds to someone of the McIlhenny family, who, planting them, had experimented with the peppers and evolved this sauce by a recipe that is to this day a family secret, to the family's considerable profit.

We found the factory. Sophy said she had accomplished this in spite of the directions. I maintained it was because there were two gentlemen standing in front of a pleasant building no one would have identified as a factory. One of the gentlemen was Mr. Walter McIlhenny, our host, and he introduced his nephew, Mr. Ned Simmons. Perhaps Mr. Simmons is a cousin. Long before we left the island I had become so confused between Averys and McIlhennys, and the other names they have married, I gave up trying to sort out the relationships.

Mr. McIlhenny told us he had wanted only to welcome us. He

could not as yet leave the factory, but Ned would show us where we were to stay and then take us to the bird sanctuary. We would meet more members of the family at dinner.

We were allowed no time to enjoy the guest house given over to us. We must hurry, Mr. Simmons urged. It was getting toward dusk. The birds would be coming in. Two men servants ran back and forth from the car to the house removing our bags. We followed on the run, too, flung open our bags, changed to walking shoes, threw off city furs, snatched up sweaters and topcoats, raced back to the car and climbed in.

Darn said a little breathlessly, "We're ready, Mr. Simmons," and drew on a pair of fresh white gloves.

It took only a few minutes to reach the place. We drove fast and for once I didn't mind. There was no traffic on these roads, and even had there been any, I was too preoccupied, I think. I don't know why I was tense with excitement, perhaps from the sense of urgency Mr. Simmons had communicated and his own anticipation.

He said to Sophy (he sat beside her), "Turn here—watch for a curve—you can push a little now," and except when he spoke to her he had his head out the window beside him and was watching the sky. "Here we are," he told her suddenly, and added almost in a shout, "We're in time. Come along."

I did notice the car was stopped beside feathery trees because I walked among them, fast, almost running, keeping up with Mr. Simmons, who led us single file along a path. We came out of this grove at the foot of a flight of steps.

Mr. Simmons pointed up. "There's the platform," he said. And we climbed to a lookout.

The platform was large; we moved about on it easily. Twice our number would not have crowded it. We leaned on a railing that encircled it and looked down below at a lake of black water, vegetation growing in it and coming thickly down to its borders.

A few birds were on the branches of trees that fringed the water. I saw two heron standing some distance from me, and beyond them I thought I saw motion in a clump of marsh weeds. "Well, there they are," I thought, the birds we had come to see, only I couldn't make them out very clearly.

Mr. Simmons had brought field glasses. They were slung over his shoulder. I asked if I might use them a minute. To my surprise he shook his head, but smiled. "No," he said, "wait." He pointed to the sky.

I looked up and saw two beautiful white birds coasting down toward us, without motion of their wings, or sound.

"Oh," I said, and found my voice was quavering, "the beauties. There they are, the egrets."

I watched them as they came silently to earth, but at the instant of their lighting Mr. Simmons spoke sharply, "Look up," he said. Fifty, seventy-five, a hundred, a thousand birds were above us suddenly within our view; white, blue, gray, black, large and small. They made no more sound in flight than a summer breeze through a clump of willows. But when they had landed on limbs and on shore, they began to talk, and I have heard such chatter only at a woman's club luncheon.

I want no ornithologist to identify or translate for me bird sounds. What we heard that evening was bird gossip. Newsy notes of the day, where everybody had been, whom they had seen, what they had picked up, and where the pickings had been good, or unsatisfactory.

The air above us was filled again and down they came, silently, and on the instant of arrival increased the clamor. Now bushes and trees and water were dotted with white. I have seen tufts of cotton left on bushes after a picking. This was like that sight, except that the white tufts were of a size I could scarcely have put my two hands around, and every tuft had antennae, a little tower of delicate filaments. This was the crown, the crest of the egret.

I didn't count the number of times the sky filled, but the birds came, again and again—sometimes a small group, twenty-five or thirty, then hundreds, and now and then stragglers or independents, by ones and twos.

"Now," Mr. Simmons said at last, "would you like the glasses?"

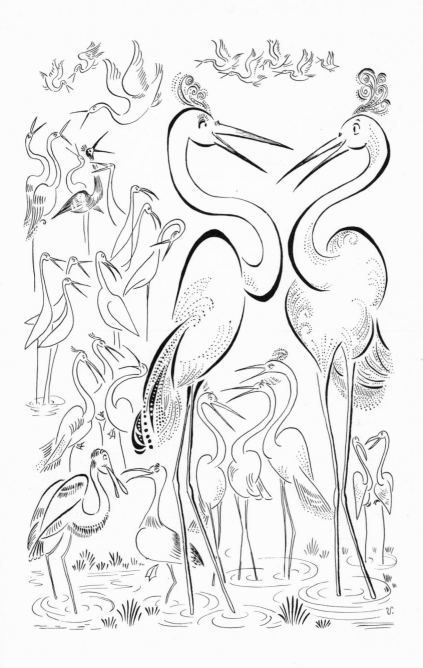

It was the first word that had been said since the birds had come. I shook my head. I didn't want the glasses now. I wanted not to be confined. I must see all the sky and all the area below. It had been a quiet place, and now everything moved and made sound.

Ellen took the glasses. And as she described, Mr. Simmons told her what she saw. "American egrets, snowy egrets, the big blue heron, the small heron. With long hooked beaks? Those are ibis. Louisiana crane, coots, redwinged blackbirds, gallinules, ducks, geese—" and more that I cannot remember.

Through the center of the lake there is a series of platforms on stilts high above the surface of the water, like a boardwalk at a summer resort, except there are no steps by which one could reach it. Pointing to it I said to Mr. Simmons, "Evidently that was made for the birds but they don't seem to care for it."

"You should see it in the spring," was his answer. "Those are the nesting platforms, and I assure you they are crowded during the season. And I'll tell you something else you really have to see to believe. Every bird family has its own apartment, you might call it, and it's crowded as a tenement; nest to nest with no space in between. But when the parent birds come home, or the male, if the female is nesting, they make no mistake about their address. They'll come down out of the sky right straight to their own apartment, not a bit of uncertainty or scrambling about, apologizing at having got off at the wrong address. Each one goes straight to his own. In all the years I've watched them, I swear I don't know how they do it."

Darn asked how long he had been watching them and how he came to know so much about them.

Mr. Simmons grinned sheepishly. "Ever since I was big enough to climb up these steps," he said, "or maybe before. Anyway as long as I can remember. When I was a child," he explained, "for a while we didn't live on the island, but I used to spend all my vacations here. I was always crazy about the birds. I've watched them from every spot, I guess, and about every time of day or night. You never get tired of them. Why don't you see them take off at dawn?" he added. "That's a wonderful sight, too."

"I'll do it," Sophy and I said simultaneously.

Kat shook her head decisively. "Not me," she said.

Ellen's voice quavered, "Really at dawn?"

Darn sighed. "I guess I know who'll have to wake you," she said resignedly.

I realized we had been talking because there were no birds coming in, and I looked inquiringly and a little startled at Mr. Simmons. He must have realized my sudden awareness of what was not happening, because he smiled and nodded his head. "That's right," he said, "it's all over. There may be a few late stragglers, but the respectable citizens are home for the night."

I think we had been there not over half an hour. I'm sure the whole flight had been within an hour. Before we left I asked if I might use the glasses since I was assured I would not miss anything overhead. I would have missed a great deal had I not used them. But I saw one pitiful sight I cannot forget. I had picked out a bird of unusual color, though it looked like an egret. Instead of a snowy white, it was a yellow beige. I asked Mr. Simmons what it could be. He took the glasses from me quickly.

"Oh Lord," he said, "I'm afraid I know." One look evidently confirmed his knowledge. "It's an egret all right," he said, "poor thing. It's been down to the Gulf and got into some oil. That's happening quite often these days and I'm afraid it's going to get worse. Sometimes they can't even make it back to the sanctuary. The oil sticks, pins their wings down. They can't fly. You can see how this fellow's trying with his bill to separate the feathers. If it isn't too bad the oil will dry a little, and I don't know whether it wears off or how they get rid of it, but sometimes they do. If they make it back here of course they have a better chance of survival because they can get food and be safe while they're recovering."

As we started down the steep stair flight, I took one last look back over the sanctuary. Twilight was close by. The blue herons were melted into a monotone of water, trees and shrubs. Only the white cotton tufts, the egrets, still gleamed out of the dim light; the pitch of chatter was lowered now to a throaty, lazy murmur and even that as I listened was fading off. As I turned again to go down the steps I had a foolish feeling of closing the door to a nursery and calling back, "Good night, children. Now settle down and no more talking." Had the stairs been not so steep I think I would have tiptoed down them.

It was a bamboo grove we'd passed through, Mr. Simmons told me when we retraced our way to the car, and it was a famous one, because of the number of varieties represented, and also because, under Mr. McIlhenny's care, they had grown so magnificently. Some, he said, measured sixty feet in height.

Riding back in the car, I said ruefully, "Somebody once said of a friend of mine, he was an 'excellent talker except that he has no terminal facilities.' I feel that way about this trip. It's an excellent trip, a marvelous trip, but it has no terminal facilities, or at least I have none about it. Everything I see I say to myself, 'I must come back to this.'"

"I don't know about the other places," Mr. Simmons answered, "but you can't make one trip to Avery Island a terminal. If you come in January you'll see the camellias at their best, and there are over ten thousand bushes in the gardens. If you come in early March you'll see the azaleas. Those come by the acre here. Then, of course, the wisteria is famous, too, and the rose gardens are something to see." He laughed apologetically. "I happen to love the place."

Darn sitting beside me spoke quietly. "We'll be back," she said.

At dinner Mr. McIlhenny told us the guest house in which we were staying had been made from two houses in the old slave quarters. The big bell that had called the slaves still swung from its pole outside. The houses were of the soft dusty rose that old brick becomes. The original houses each made a bedroom wing in the guest house, and the two were joined by a long living room-dining room, opening in the front onto a patio, and in the back looking, by way of a window that ran almost the length of the room, on sloping lawn and a running stream. Ellen and Kat had taken over one bedroom wing, Darn, Sophy and I the other.

Dressed for dinner, we had come almost simultaneously into the big room and found Mr. McIlhenny just arrived and about to mix cocktails. Miss Katherine Avery came in soon after and then Mrs. Simmons, gay and pretty, but a little uneasy because she had allowed her husband to stay at home and baby sit, since we'd been with him in the afternoon. They were without a maid or nurse, she explained, and he'd volunteered to do it. But she wasn't sure she was right to let him, and she wasn't "right sure he'd do it right."

Mr. McIlhenny put a cocktail into her hand and she said, thanking him, she guessed she wouldn't worry any more.

I was telling our host how we loved the guest house, and though there was certainly nothing whimsy about it, it did have a kind of fairytale quality.

Darn joined the conversation endorsing my sentiments and she added, "Will you tell me what that tremendous basin is in the patio that the fountain drips into? I never saw anything like it. Goodness knows *it's* real enough; it looks as though it were made of iron. But what is it?"

Mr. McIlhenny was pleased by her bewilderment. "I don't wonder you're confused about it," was his answer. "You wouldn't find one of those in other parts of the country. It's a sugar kettle, one of the old ones for melting down the cane when it used to be done by hand. Now the big machines have taken over, and the co-operative plants, of course, use receptacles about fifty times this size. Lately people have been buying up the old ones for just such things as this or for their gardens, but there are still some of them around."

"Where would you go to look for them?" was Darn's next question, and as Mr. McIlhenny was answering her, Sophy strolled over to our little group. She reached us, as Darn, pulling a notebook and pencil from her evening bag, asked another question, and prepared to jot down the answer. "Could you give me the name of that reliable junkyard?" was her query.

"Oh mercy God," Sophy said, and walked away again.

A few minutes later the conversation became general and Sophy explained to Miss Avery a little of the trouble she was having with her friends, because, she said, "They keep wanting to buy things and I'm the one who has to load the car. The rear view is almost entirely blocked off now. The last corner of it would have been covered over if Emily had bought the rug and bedspread she was looking at in St. Martinville."

Miss Avery turned eagerly to me. "Oh," she said, "if you like these hand-woven things I'd love to take you tomorrow to see some of them here. I know an old lady who does her own spinning as well as weaving and really makes beautiful things; blankets, bedspreads, rugs."

Ellen and Darn, overhearing this, added their enthusiastic acceptance to mine.

"Can't I ever keep my big mouth shut?" Sophy muttered, but I heard her.

Dinner was served to us in the main room of the guest house on little individual tables as we gathered around the fire. That is, the first course of creamed oysters was served to us. Then we moved to the buffet table under the big window, heaped high with food. From that I ate shrimp and rice, sweet potatoes laced with sherry, green salad, and for dessert a chocolate pie that had in it, of all things, a touch of brandy, and was magnificent. The pie, however, was the only thing that had not a touch of Tabasco sauce, and I may say parenthetically that since my return home I am the hostess with the bottle of Tabasco upended and dispensed over nearly every dish.

We heard more at dinner about the background of Avery Island—how the member of the family who took possession settled there in 1793. People had a habit, Mr. McIlhenny said, of settling there once they'd arrived at the island. He told us of a guest who'd come for a two-day visit and had stayed the remainder of his life, and, Mr. McIlhenny added, he had lived to be a very old man. Even after he had died he hadn't gone back to the place from which he had originated. He was buried in the cemetery on Avery.

Miss Avery captured Kat's attention. She said Kat might be particularly interested in the story of an ancestor named Juliette, because Juliette was the great-grandmother of Kat's husband.

Word had reached the family, so the story runs, that Juliette on a visit to Paris had danced with Lafayette. The family opinion of this episode, received some time later in a letter, was indifferent to the person with whom she had danced, but concerned with the dance itself and ran, in effect, as follows: "Dearest Juliette,—If you love delicacy, promise us you will never waltz again."

"My dear," Ellen said to Kat when the story had been told, "that's undoubtedly why Juliette's great-grandson married you, a Bostonian."

Mr. McIlhenny and his lady relatives left not long after dinner.

"You're all tired, we know," Miss Avery explained, "and I understand you're getting up to see the bird flight in the morning. After that there's a lot I'd like to show you. And Walter wants to take you around."

He endorsed this and added, "Suppose I come down here for breakfast about half past eight, how would that do?"

We told him it would do beautifully. Kat, Ellen and Darn assured him, he would find them ready for breakfast. Sophy and I looked at each other and agreed with a nod we would still keep to our plan, and announced this aloud, at the same time forbidding Darn to rouse herself in order to waken us. No congratulations came to us for our stamina; only from our friends an urgent request to make no noise on our departure. They wanted to see or hear nothing of us until we met at breakfast. We promised to observe these requests, and we did observe them.

We made no noise whatever until I, emerging from sleep at the sound of a knock at my door, called, "What is it?"

The door opened, a pleasant colored maid came in carrying a tray. "It's eight o'clock, lady," she said. "I brought you some orange juice and coffee. Mr. McIlhenny will be here at half past eight. The other ladies are dressing themselves. They thought maybe you'd like to be wakened."

Chapter Fifteen

"HOW ARE YOU ALL THIS MORNING?" WAS MISS AVERY'S greeting when she picked us up after breakfast for the tour.

Kat answered, "Fine," she said, "wonderful. We slept like babies. Sophy and Emily didn't wake up in time to see the birds fly out. Emily was a little short-tempered about that, but she ate an enormous breakfast and since then she's been in fine form. Gay as a cricket."

There is no use hoping Kat will keep her perceptiveness to herself, but she was perfectly right. However frequently I may think of myself in my fantasy life as a creature of fire, air and dew, in my moments of realistic appraisal, I know there have been very few times in my life when, after an emotional disturbance, large or small, my equilibrium is not restored, or at least perceptibly improved by good food. That morning I had been disgruntled at missing the early flight of the birds. But after I had nibbled heartily some stewed, spiced pears, tiny sausages, samp, hot biscuits with jam, I'd recovered remarkably, and was ready for the next round of sights.

It began with a visit to the pepper fields. They spread over many acres. That morning the acres were peopled with colored women workers who moved up and down the rows of plants, picking the small, bright orange fruit. For protection from the sun, they wore bandannas of bright colors, wrapped tight around their heads. Their cotton dresses were in many colored prints. The warm sun intensified the shades in the shifting kaleidoscope. Half closing my eyes against the glare I lost the individuals and saw only a shimmering movement of color.

We traveled over the greater part of the island after we left the pepper field, and as she drove, Miss Avery, when I questioned her, told something of the work she has done there and in the nearby community off the island. In spite of the protests of her family at such independence—this was a number of years ago—she had taken nurses' training and put it to work in social service among the Cajuns.

We stopped at some of the houses that members of the family who have left the island come back to occupy in the holidays. Each one of these has a superb view because the island rises high above the surrounding countryside. I yearned over, even coveted, a beautiful building that was not inhabited. It wasn't even a house, Miss Avery told me, when I exclaimed over it. It was an old sugar mill that had not been in operation for years and was slowly disintegrating. I insisted the proportions and architectural simplicity would make it a very satisfying place in which to live, but my real covetousness was for the bricks, soft, dusty rose, like those in the guest house and so many houses of this Louisiana countryside through which we had passed.

Sophy sitting beside me shuddered and spoke. "Hold on to the bricks, Miss Avery," she said, "I beg of you, or she'll pile as many as she can get into the station wagon, Lord knows what for in a New York apartment, but I'm thinking of the station wagon. It doesn't belong to us. We've only rented it."

Ellen came into the conversation dreamily. "I could use them," she said. "They'd be lovely. I know just the place for them. We're building a new house in the country," she added in explanation to Miss Avery.

Sophy addressed herself, too, to our driver. "Miss Avery," she asked earnestly, "could I ask you to drive us off the island?"

We left the island but that brought small comfort to Sophy, because Miss Avery took us to call on Mrs. Dronath in the nearby village of Erath. Mrs. Dronath was the Acadian who did the spinning and weaving Miss Avery had told us about the night before. We were delighted to meet her, and to see her spinning wheel, her loom and their products. She spoke no English and her

French was difficult to understand, but this was no obstacle to our purchasing some of the lovely things she had made. I bought a soft white rug for a grandchild's room, a baby blanket, some guest towels, and I think Sophy was not so morose over my bundles as over the discovery that she herself had bought some articles.

We returned to the island in time to meet Mr. McIlhenny by appointment at the entrance to the salt mine that is another of the family's industries. We made the descent from the mouth of the mine in an elevator that swayed a little and in total impenetrable darkness. No one in our group mentioned any sense of uneasiness. No one mentioned anything. Not a word was spoken. I would not have been surprised to learn my friends, like me, were praying.

We stepped out into a vast labyrinthian underground area, with soft white walls and high ceiling overhead, all salt of course. Mr. Jay served as our guide. He was an officer of the salt mine company to whom Mr. McIlhenny had introduced us above ground. Mr. Jay, leading the way from the elevator, put us into a jeep nearby. Our numbers necessitated an unconventional seating arrangement. For Mr. McIlhenny to be included, he was not actually in the car but straddling the hood, and assured us it was a place he frequently assumed when he was host to a group of visitors. We drove bumpily and rapidly along wide passages that turned and twisted. There was no work going on because it was the lunch hour, so that apart from the unearthly quality the soft whiteness of the walls and roof gave to the place, there was added the eeriness of total absence of sound other than of our motor and our voices. I can now say I have seen a salt mine but I was profoundly thankful to be above ground again.

I was much happier in the jungle garden; more than that I was spellbound by the beauty of those acres, more than two hundred of them, all landscaped, with sunken garden, pools and stream. The temple garden is somewhere in this acreage. Well-marked signs guide the tourist to all of these spots, and the temple garden is one that must not be overlooked. Its center is a Chinese temple that holds within it a magnificent statue of Buddha. This is reflected in the mirror of a lagoon below, where Chinese lotus grows. There was not nearly enough time to explore. Already we were coming to the hour when, by agreement with Clara and Emma, we would pick them up in New Iberia and resume our schedule.

We lunched at the guest house and were joined there by other members of the family: Mrs. Ringle, and Mrs. Simmons, the mother of our bird guide, Ned. If ladies in the South habitually lunch as we lunched in that part of the country, then there must be a profound difference between Northern and Southern body chemistry that allows them to maintain their slim figures. Our luncheon on Avery Island included fried chicken, broiled mushrooms on top of squares of golden brown grits, creamed spinach, grapefruit salad, hot rolls, and for dessert thin pancakes rolled around jelly and served with a rum sauce.

During lunch we learned Mrs. Simmons' specialty is cattle, and that she has a fine herd. The beginning of the herd and her occupation was a Brahman bull her father, Mr. McIlhenny, had bought in India. The bull had arrived in a hand-woven bamboo crate. Container and contents won Mrs. Simmons' heart. She feeds her bulls, she told us, three hundred loaves of bread twice a week. She buys up the stale loaves from bakeries over a considerable area.

I asked if this was a diet used by all breeders. She told me she thought it was not, but that she herself had found it highly successful.

The figure that waved and danced on the sidewalk as we drove up to the Frederick Hotel in New Iberia denies my theory of a special Southern chemistry; it is ample and it belongs to Rosa Hart, the wonderful dynamo of Lake Charles, and my friend. She was the friend of Ellen, Kat, Darn and Sophy within five minutes of their introduction. By comparison with Rosa's, Emma Michie's vitality and energy are as a lagoon to a millrace and I was thankful that my dear companions had met Emma first.

Simultaneously with the introduction of my friends to Rosa, she was introducing to us a young man who had come with her from Lake Charles and of whose name I never became sure. I know that he is a merchant seaman, that he was at that time having a holiday in Lake Charles between ships, that he is one of Rosa's many protégés, and he hopes one day to write. I think his name is Fred Smith. I call him that, and I shall be grateful to him "for keeps" as the children say, because without him and the arrangements he made, we would not have seen a *fais do do*. The *fais do do* was at night and in Mamou.

Before that time and place we went to call on Mr. Weeks Hall at his beautiful old house, "Shadows on the Teche" in New Iberia. Clara and Emma were with us again. We now numbered nine. I joined the station-wagon group in order to take over from Kat the leadership she had assumed on Avery Island and do a bit of briefing and coaching myself. I had planned to tell them about Rosa before we reached Lake Charles, not wanting to tax their capacity for absorbing information by giving them too much about too many people at the outset.

"But," I began, "who would have thought Rosa would come from Lake Charles to New Iberia in order to take us back to Lake Charles?" I corrected myself. "Why wouldn't I have thought of it? If Clara and Emma came all the way to New Orleans, why wouldn't I have expected Rosa to meet us in New York and bring us all the way? Everything about her," I insisted, "is on a large scale—her generosity, her imagination, her drive, and certainly her list of friends."

I told them about The Lake Charles Little Theatre that is really Rosa's theater, and is known all over the country, not because it was written about in *Life* Magazine as "One of America's livelier experiments in cultural democracy," but because Rosa has made it a place to which theater lovers come from astonishing distances. She produces, casts, directs the plays presented there, paints scenery, gathers properties and puts out publicity. When she is casting, and I have heard this from many and reliable sources, there is no citizen of Lake Charles who, leaving his bed in the morning, can feel any assurance he will return to it that night at his customary hour. He may very well be, instead, on the stage of Rosa's theater, a script of the coming play in his hand, shouts and bellows from Rosa in his ears, and his name recorded in the cast of characters. This has happened many times. A delivery boy bringing a package to the theater was signed up before he returned to his shop. A bank official consulted in his office at noon one day for advice about financial matters pertaining to the little theater was at 9 P.M. on the acting side of the footlights, script in hand.

"By the way," I added, as we drew up behind the other car, "Rosa also runs a bookshop; the name of it is the '3 R's,' standing for Readin', Ritin' and Rosa."

We arrived at "Shadows on the Teche." I would have passed it because I was not looking for a plantation on the corner of Main and Weeks Streets in New Iberia. Had I caught sight of the house itself, I would have put on the brakes, stopped in my tracks and whistled with pleasure; but the house cannot be seen from the street; it is protected by a high thick hedge of bamboo.

Happily, any traveler may go into the grounds and the house. They are open to the public, with certain restrictions that Mr. Weeks Hall has posted. "Groups of four feet tall and up," his sign reads, "house and grounds sixty cents each, gardens twenty-five cents each." Evidently if a child has not grown up to a stature of four feet, he is not welcome.

"The Shadows" includes my two favorite ingredients for house building: dusty rose brick and Doric columns across the front. There are also two galleries and connecting them an outside stairway at the far end to the left of the lower gallery as one faces the house.

Rosa urged us to see the gardens first, because, she said, once you meet Weeks Hall you won't want to stop talking with him to look at any other scenery. We accepted her suggestion and visited first the garden, finding without surprise it is a lovely spot, and that each of its four corners is punctuated by a statue of one of the seasons. Rosa took us to the far side of the house, and this faces the Bayou Teche, but is on a bank twenty feet or so above the water. I consider such a situation bewildering and said as much to Rosa and the other Southern representatives.

"I think it's beautiful," I told them, "and I love seeing the water through the oak trees and the shadows they make, but I thought a bayou was a bayou because it runs between banks that are level with it. What are we doing standing twenty feet above a bayou?"

They soothed me with words about this being very unusual and one of the features of "Shadows on the Teche."

As we turned back toward the house, sunlight on a copper spout caught my attention. I paused to look and saw there were two of them, and that one carried the initials D.W. and the other the date 1830.

Rosa was a little impatient at my stopping. She seemed uneasy. Tugging at my sleeve she said, "Come on, now, Weeks is going to be mad if we don't get up to see him and he'll blame me for keeping you all so long."

I moved on with the others and as we came round again to the street side of the house, we heard a rapid staccato of vigorous pounding from above and looked at one another and at Rosa inquiringly.

She nodded her head. "That's right," she said, "that's Weeks, and he's mad."

I started quickly for the front door, but Rosa again put her hand on my arm. "No," she told me, "not that way. We go up. He had a bad accident a while back. It's left him sort of incapacitated. He lives upstairs." She motioned me toward the outer stairway at the end of the gallery.

I climbed it but stopped on the turn at the sight of a mirror on a bracket from the wall there. "Why good gracious," I said, and called softly down to Sophy, "Wait till you see this, a Philadelphia busybody here."

A strong voice came down from above me. "That's exactly what it is, so I can see if a person coming up is somebody I want to wait for or run out on. Come along, now, come along. I wish Rosa had stayed at home. I'm not going to speak to her, herding you all over the place. You're supposed to be calling on me, not my garden. Did you like it?"

I had reached him and as he talked we were shaking hands. Rosa was behind me. "Hush," she told him, "stop fussing."

He dropped my hand to embrace her affectionately. When he had released her she introduced the others as each came up the stairs. When she had finished, I added, "And my name is Emily Kimbrough, since no one has introduced us."

"Didn't matter, didn't matter," was the answer. "You're a friend of Rosa's. That's enough."

He led us along the upper gallery, leaning heavily on the cane with which he had been violently thumping the floor a few minutes earlier. We followed him through an austere, beautiful drawing room, and as we passed them he waved his cane at two portraits on the wall. "Sightseers always ask who those portraits are. Such nonsense. Who cares what people's names are? I tell them those are portraits of Martha Washington and Abraham Lincoln, who lived together in sin here."

"What *are* their names?" Darn asked. "I'm a sightseer."

Rosa gave Mr. Hall an affectionate shove that very nearly up-ended him, saying, "That's one for you, my boy." And to Darn, "They're his great-grandparents, or maybe great-greats."

We drank coffee from tiny silver cups in a comfortable sitting room behind the salon. Sophy and I talked with Mr. Hall about mutual friends in Philadelphia, and when Darn asked him questions about the house he answered them meekly and accurately. That it had been built in 1830 on what was then the large estate of his ancestor, David Weeks, that almost all the woodwork is the original and of Louisiana cypress, and that the blinds are also unchanged after more than a century.

Kat and Ellen at his invitation saw the other rooms on the second floor and from the upper gallery looked down on the garden below. When they returned they reported enthusiastically an engaging portrait of a child on a bedroom wall.

"That's my mother," Weeks Hall said quickly, "in case you'd like to know who it is," and made a little face at Darn.

What fun it had been and how generous of him to have welcomed so many of us, we told him as we got up to leave. He followed us to the head of the outer stairs, urging us to return. "But without Rosa," he added, and embraced her again.

Rosa took charge when we reached our cars. "Now then," she said briskly, "we'll go straight to Opelousas for dinner. Didee's is the best place to eat. It's only a step from here. And then as soon as we've had dinner, we'll run on over to Mamou for the *fais do do*, and after that it's just nothing at all to Lake Charles. I don't want you all to get tired right at the beginning, so I've planned it easy."

The step from New Iberia to Opelousas took about two hours. I daresay the distance can be covered in a little less time. We were held up by the almost interminable lines of slow-moving trucks piled with cane. As it was, Clara's car, in which I was a passenger, was ahead of the station wagon that included Rosa. Had she not mentioned the name of the restaurant, I don't know that we would have come together again that evening. But we remembered Didee's and found it. The other carload came twenty minutes or so after our arrival.

The menu at Didee's offers a wide choice, but suddenly all of us craved food that had a simple taste and was without sauce. We had scrambled eggs, bacon and toast.

The next step, to Mamou, took over an hour. Again we didn't drive fast. This time it was because Clara said that once driving on a country road like this in the dark, she'd hit a cow and hadn't liked it. The cow's dislike had been even more acute. The cow had died.

The main street of Mamou at night looked like a scene from an old silent movie of a Western town. It was wide. I daresay it is wide in the daytime, too, but that night along its curbs was an assortment of vehicles I would have thought only Hollywood could have assembled as props. There were several kinds of horse-drawn carriages, each horse nodding into a feed bag. One

drew a covered buggy, another an open cart, a third a two-seated carriage, and there were duplicates of these models. I saw a Model T Ford and the newest Cadillac. What I did not see was an open parking space. The Cajuns had come to town for their *fais do do.*

Clara drove slowly looking for a place but stopped at the sound of Sophy's horn behind us, and we all looked back. Sophy was beckoning us to follow. She pulled around ahead of us and turned into a side street.

Three people stood on the sidewalk, evidently waiting for us. They waved at our approach and pointed to two parking places. When we joined them we were introduced by Fred to one of the group called O.C. I learned later his name is José, but that to the Cajuns he was O.C. He and Fred had worked together on a tanker, but O.C. was a native Mamoun. O.C. introduced us to his companions, Mr. Reed and a Mrs. Reed, who was not his wife. Mr. Reed in fact had not met her before this evening. She was a reporter on a newspaper in a nearby town and O.C. had invited her to join us. I further discovered it was from Rosa to Fred to O.C. that the evening had been accomplished. All this was in our conversation as we walked back to the main street. When we reached it O.C. stopped in front of a lighted store, looked a little anxiously from one to the other of us, and respectfully asked if we would gather close around him, so that he might tell us a few things. We huddled in a football playing clump, and O.C. in his Cajun English—and I cannot reproduce it—explained that at Mamou there are two halls for a *fais do do*: one for the old folks, the other a few doors down the street for the young people. We would visit each. The Cajuns were happy to have guests but did not like them to stare like sightseers that came in just to look. "Like at freaks. You see?" O.C. asked apologetically.

We assured him we did indeed, and wanted to do only what would be the least conspicuous.

O.C. grinned with relief. "Then we all go now," he suggested happily.

We crossed the street. There was no traffic moving on it.

Obviously everybody was already there. We entered a building a few doors to our left. It was a one-story structure, the inside of rough wood. It, too, looked like a bar and dancehall from an early Western movie. The bar was the first room we entered off the street and it was crowded with standees several rows deep. We edged our way round them, and through a doorway into the room beyond that was the dancehall. There were tables and chairs around the edge of this and it was crowded, too, but O.C. led us all the way to the far end and found an empty table there just under the musicians' stand. We made a parade of some length, moving single file, but we attracted, I could see, no particular attention.

We had arrived during an intermission. We were no sooner seated than the music began again. Old-fashioned fiddle music, it was, the bows scraping the strings, harshly but vigorously, the melody unfamiliar. O.C. was standing behind me. He had chosen not to sit down; he wanted to keep an eye on everything going on, he explained.

He leaned down and spoke close to my ear. Above the music it was hard to hear him. "They play old French tunes," he said, "all Cajun music, especially 'Big Mamou.'"

After a few bars of the music the room began to fill. I saw O.C. had not exaggerated when he said the *fais do dos* in this hall were for the older folk. Though there were young couples, there were elderly people, too. Hands are not twisted and joints swollen from working only a few years. These faces were lined, the skin thickened by many seasons of labor in the sun. But the dancers carried themselves well and their feet were light on the floor. They did not combine in square dancing; they danced in couples. Here and there one showed off a few fancy steps, but for the most part they went round and round in a sort of two-step in quick time with much arm pumping. There was no cutting in, but the music stopped frequently for a general change of partners.

I beckoned O.C. and he leaned down again. "Am I right," I asked him, "that these people have worked all day and they'll dance here all night, and go back to work again? And they do this twice a week?"

O.C. shrugged his shoulders. "But of course, madame," he said, "they do not stop the work, but they must have fun to live, isn't it?"

"Yes," I said, "it is. It's wonderful."

Two of my friends caused a little trouble. Sophy became suddenly somewhat carried away by the music, and rising to her feet executed a little jig. This brought attention to our corner and I was forced to hiss at her to sit down. She complied instantly but regretfully, and I leaned forward to whisper to her, "I'm sorry, but they think you're imitating them. O.C. says so."

Sophy was chagrined. Nothing had been farther from her mind, she told O.C. across my shoulder, but she'd understood him to say anybody could dance, and the music had made her feel like dancing.

O.C. shrugged his shoulders again apologetically. "Generally it is two people."

A heavy-set, red-faced gentleman stood in front of Sophy and bowing offered her a glass of red wine, and with it simultaneously an invitation in French to dance.

Kat's voice cut through, sharp and clear, "Now, Sophy, you see, we can't have this."

Ellen's voice broke in. "Oh, isn't that lovely," she said, "I do hope you will, dear."

But Sophy was abashed, and though we prodded her, refused the offer politely, but firmly.

A few minutes later I saw we were again attracting attention; passing couples nudged one another and turned toward us. I followed the direction in which they were looking and saw at once the focal point of their interest. It was a bright focus: Darn's white gloves. She was pulling over her hands a fresh pair.

O.C. simultaneously saw what was happening and spoke in my ear again. "They don't wear gloves at *fais do dos*."

I turned the suggestion into an order. "Take off those gloves. They're blinding everybody."

Darn peeled them off immediately and was so dismayed at having made a gaff, she half rose and tucked the gloves underneath her, evidently to make sure they were completely out of sight. A few minutes later she sat on her hands, too, probably because having embarrassed others by her gloves, she embarrassed herself without them.

O.C. suggested we might like to visit the other dancehall, and at the next intermission, Kat, Darn, Ellen, Sophy and I filed out behind O.C., the others deciding to stay where they were and hold our places.

The young people's *fais do do* was only a few doors away from the one we had just left. O.C. said this was to allow parents to keep an eye on their young and yet slip to the other hall for a few rounds themselves. A row of sheets made a curtain on the right of the entry. A couple parted these, and came out. Behind them and the curtains I saw a bar. Fred explained the State was going through a "clean-up" movement that had threatened to be troublesome for the *fais do dos*, because by law no children may enter a bar. But the Cajuns had resolved the difficulty by cutting off the bar by means of the line of sheets we saw. Presumably, this created for minors an impenetrable barrier. Fred also said the Cajuns had been surprised to learn of the repeal of Prohibition. They hadn't heard about Prohibition.

In the dancehall proper, benches against the wall circled the room. We could see through a door at the far end a little ice-cream parlor with boys and girls at tables having innocuous refreshments of sodas, Coke and the like.

The music began, the youngsters left their tables and in a minute the dance floor was crowded. Though I saw many on the floor who looked eighteen and a little over, I saw a good number I would have guessed to be not more than nine or ten.

O.C. confirmed my estimate. "They start at the very young," he told me, "and is very good reason for this. Mamas and papas bringing their boys and girls and looking at boys and girls from the other mamas and papas for making marriages. That is why you see mamas and papas all here, so nothing can go bad. But also so something can come good for future."

I asked what the mamas and papas did with their littler ones.

"Wait till music stop," O.C. said, "then take quick look down under benches."

I repeated this suggestion to my friends. When the music stopped we ducked our heads quickly, taking a surreptitious look. We saw the littlest ones, each rolled in a blanket. Babies were sleeping on the floor beneath the benches. The next older ones, O.C. said, were in rows on the floor in a room upstairs. "All family here," he added. "Nobody left behind."

The music began again. The dancers rushed to the floor. Their style was considerably more gymnastic than that of their elders up the street. There was nowhere for us to sit. We were in some peril from the arms and legs gyrating around us.

We returned to the more conservative gathering, what Sophy termed, "The Philadelphia Assembly" of the *fais do do*. We entered during an intermission and found a newcomer at our table. Emma introduced us all as friends without bothering about names. The new arrival was Cajun, speaking only French. She was handsome, only moderately tall but with a straight slim figure, clear smooth skin, bright blue eyes and a pompadour of hair almost as white as Darn's gloves. She wore a straight black dress and over it a bright red sweater.

Within a few minutes she had told us a good deal about herself, that she was in her seventies, she did not care to say just where in them, that she had been a widow for a considerable length of time but had begun to be tired of that single state, and had decided to come into town to look about for a husband. There were not many to be had, but there was some selection.

I asked if she would like to tell us how she would set about making her choice.

She bowed to me graciously and answered in French, "You would perhaps like to see?"

We assured her we would like it very much.

"Then watch," she told us, and rose from the table. She walked to an adjoining one and with a regal nod of the head and charming smile said to the group seated there, "You will permit? I shall return it untouched." As she said this she picked up a wine glass filled nearly to the brim with red wine, and with another nod turned and walked out on the dance floor.

"Play, if you please," she ordered in a firm commanding voice to the musicians on the platform. "A waltz."

Obediently, the musicians picked up their instruments, the leader stamped on the floor a few beats to mark the tempo, and the orchestra swung into a waltz.

Our friend bowed to each corner of the room much like Queen Elizabeth in the ceremony of her coronation, and then slowly raising the glass of wine, set it carefully on the top of her head. When it was placed there to her satisfaction, she withdrew her hand and began to waltz, slowly, and in perfect rhythm, turning this way and that, sometimes completely around. She circled the room. When she had returned to her starting point, she stopped,

lifted her hand, removed the glass of wine, bowed again to the musicians. The music stopped. She walked to the table from which she had taken it, set the glass down in its original place, faced the room again and with a ravishing smile called out *"Voilà."*

Pandemonium was the accolade she received—cheers, shouts, handclappings, stamping on the floor. We rose from our table simultaneously. No one of us needed to say to another, "This is the peak. Let's go remembering this."

We were able to reach her before the rest of the room closed in. *"Magnifique,"* we told her, and thanked her *"mille fois"* for a superb performance.

She acknowledged our tributes graciously and then added with a gamin's wink, "And now you see how it will be."

At the door we turned back and saw how it was: a queen making her selection from among her subjects begging from her any small favor she might bestow.

Chapter Sixteen

LAKE CHARLES WAS FOR US A CARROUSEL THAT WE RODE giddily, and there was not just one brass ring to snatch; favors were dropped into our laps on every whirlaround. Never were such hospitable, warm-hearted, gay hosts.

We didn't come into town with Rosa, Emma, Clara and Fred after the *fais do do*. We puny Northerners had taken as many of Rosa's steps as we had strength for I told her as we came out of the dancehall. "One more and we'll all fall down."

Rosa could scarcely believe this announcement. "Why, honey," she'd said, "it's only eighty-five miles from Mamou to Lake Charles. And it's only midnight, too. Why we'll hardly get to talking before we'll be there."

A sepulchral groan from Kat behind me had let me know how she felt about any more talking. I had therefore been firm and the Louisiana ladies, tolerant and understanding, told us we were to do exactly what we felt like and no more. This is precisely what we had done. We had retraced our steps a few miles to the town of Eunice, and at its outskirts stopped at the Oleander Motel, clean and comfortable.

The following morning we'd arrived in Lake Charles, fresh and rested but a little later than we had anticipated, because a doorknob of the Oleander had dropped into my hand. Had I been on the outside of the cottage ready to leave when this happened, the disintegration of the fixture would have been of no matter. But I was on the inside, as usual the last one ready for breakfast on account of my long hair, and no one ever waited for me. I was

alone, and turning the door handle to leave on the run for the
dining room where the others were assembled, I'd pulled off the
handle. I hallooed, banged and pounded but nobody heard me.
In the end I'd got out through a window. I'd been subjected to
further indignity when I reached the dining room and told my
friends of my predicament, with no one to help me. There were
gentle but confusing reproaches—from Ellen to the effect that if
I were ready at the time the others were, doorknobs would not
come off in my hand, and an unfriendly suggestion from Sophy
that I had now successfully shut off the normal re-entry to our
cottage. I could return as I had come, by way of the window, and
hand bags out to her for stowing in the station wagon. It still
seems to me unreasonable that, complying with this preposterous
request, I should have been chided for not slinging out the bags
more briskly.

However, we were in happy amity when we reached Lake
Charles. The day was bright and warm and at the Charleston
Hotel we were not only expected, we were welcomed. Our rooms
were waiting. They were comfortable and from them we looked
down on the lake, aquamarine in the sunlight. We were due
within an hour at a luncheon. Accordingly, after a brief appreciation of the view, each snatched from her bag the dress she would
wear to the party, hung it in the bathroom on the rod that holds
the shower curtain and turned on the hot water in the tub, to
steam out the wrinkles. Waiting for this metamorphosis to take
place we unpacked the rest of our belongings, wandering back
and forth among the rooms in conversation.

Kat commented on this. It seemed odd to her, she said, that no
matter how many hours we drove together in the station wagon,
we seemed always to have more things to say to one another when
we had achieved separate rooms. After a pause she added that on
the whole she liked it except at times when she wanted to take a
nap. This happened not to be one of those times.

Darn observed the thing she liked best about the proximity of
our hotel rooms wherever we had been was not so much the
coziness as the opportunity it had given her to learn my trick of

steaming dresses. If in New Orleans she'd been down the hall from me, instead of in an adjoining room, she wouldn't have seen me unpack, hang and steam. She supposed I'd learned this trick on lecture tours. I agreed this was so and was happy to contribute a little to her store of knowledge. Darn's degree of enjoyment is always in direct ratio to what practical benefit she has derived.

The luncheon was at Mrs. Dees'. I had been feted there on my other trip to Lake Charles and I looked forward to seeing her again. I had whetted the anticipation of my friends, too. "Wait," I told them, "until you taste her specialty."

Mrs. Dees' specialty is orange pecan candy, "Ann Dees Orange Pecans" it is called, and she ships it all over the country. It can be ordered from her at 823 Ford Street, Lake Charles. It comes in two size boxes, one pound for $2 postpaid, two pounds $3.50. I like to shout that news abroad, because there is no candy I know with such a delicate, subtle flavor. There are few things for which to thank the Depression, but this is one of them, as Mrs. Dees has told me her story. Times were hard, two little boys were to be educated, she had no business training, no particular talent she could, in the emergency, call to use. And then she'd remembered an old family recipe for a candy that for years she had made at Christmastime and given to her friends until they had come to expect and demand it. She turned it into a business.

Luncheon and the other guests were delightful as I had known both would be. But the particular joy was to see again the warm vivacious Ann Dees herself. I asked her to show Darn her collection of beautiful cups and saucers she has gathered over many years and countries. This provided a mutual pleasure between Mrs. Dees and Darn, who loves and collects china, too. Mrs. Dees assured her the only other person seeing the collection who had displayed a knowledge comparable with Darn's was Sally Rand. She had been brought to the Dees house when she had come to Lake Charles on tour. It had been a real disappointment, Mrs. Dees said, that Miss Rand had not been able to return as she had promised at Mrs. Dees' cordial invitation, because the day following her first performance her show had been closed.

We visited the "3 R's" bookshop after lunch and were reluctant to leave it because every one of us found things exactly to her taste. Only Rosa could achieve such variety in so small a space, and also such overflowing haphazard arrangement.

We dined at the Blackstone Restaurant on Highway 90. It is new and run by Alex Petter, who knows good food and provides it. Our meal began with shrimp rémoulade, progressed through cream of cabbage soup to tenderloin of beef, the slices on artichoke bottoms, surrounded with broiled mushrooms. With this course we were served broccoli and little potatoes baked in foil, and a sauterne. We ended with ice cream and crème de menthe, and coffee of course. Our hosts were Dr. and Mrs. Conway Magee. I had not known them on the earlier trip. I was a little surprised that the invitation from these strangers had been urgent, and urgently furthered by Rosa. None of us expressed any reluctance about accepting the invitation, but we did wonder to one another why there seemed to be overtones of such anxiety lest we should not come.

With the arrival of our demitasses we learned the reason for the urgency and the anxiety. Dr. Magee got up from the table, left the room and returned almost immediately, rolling, with the help of a waiter, a table on which stood a screen for showing slides. They placed the table a few feet from where we sat. Dr. Magee and the waiter then brought in a projector and set it up. The lights in the dining room were turned off. The doctor inserted a slide, and on the screen there appeared a superb photograph of a strange and wonderful place I had talked about in a book about a trip to Italy. I had called this place "The Mystery View." Dr. and Mrs. Magee had just returned from Italy and on that trip had tracked down and photographed "The Mystery View." I was momentarily speechless with astonishment. The Magees were delighted at my astonishment. Within a few seconds we were chattering like excited children. All too soon Rosa was tugging at my sleeve and telling me we must move on to the theater.

The Lake Charles Little Theatre, where for twenty-eight years

Rosa has shouted productions into shape, has been made from an old Wells Fargo stable and it is a rewarding place to see. Delightful reminders of the stable have been emphasized in its decoration, the colors are gay, the seats are comfortable. There is a patio that runs along one side of the building, where coffee is served during intermission and parties held after first nights. We were given a special performance of Edna St. Vincent Millay's *Aria da Capo,* presented by a cast of children; not a difficult cast to remember since it comprised, apart from one Jelks Jones, daughter of former Governor Jones, members of one family, the Macdonalds, the youngest eight, the oldest about sixteen. They gave a good performance.

My friends gave them and me assurance of this. I would have thought it good had they given an indifferent one. I was in a happy glow over the performance that had preceded theirs. The Mayor and I had been the entire cast. His Honor, Mayor Sidney Gray, had called me to the stage and presented, with a charming speech, a key to the city. Such a thing had never happened to me before, and my friends were gratifyingly sympathetic to my happy surprise. All of them except Sophy. She arrived just in time for the other performance, *Aria da Capo.*

In the darkness before the curtain rose, she slipped into a seat beside me, and whispered, "I heard the Mayor was going to give you a key to the city, and you'd be asked to speak in reply. So I stayed on at the restaurant and talked to Fred."

Emma had a party for us next day at lunch in her house a few miles out of town. We numbered fifteen guests, and Emma made us feel we were a cozy group of four or five. She drew us all together into animated general conversation, astonishing me once more with her extraordinary gift for making friends of strangers, almost at the moment of introduction.

Ex-Governor and Mrs. Sam Jones were among the old friends Emma had invited. He was modest about his part in it, but not reluctant to talk about the breakdown of Huey Long's power. "The Cajuns had a lot to do with it," he said among other things. "A Cajun doesn't get mad easily, but when he does, he gets terrible mad and he fights. Eventually they all got terrible mad at the machine, and they fought. Organizing is no trouble for them. They're always organized in the sense that the individual is part of the group: his friends of the *bourré* game, his fellow workers on the shrimp boat, in the cane field, the grinding mills, the rice plantation, fur trapping, whatever."

At Mamou I had listed some Cajun expressions Mrs. Reed had given me, and some I'd heard O.C. use. I quoted them because Governor Jones likes to collect them, too. He endorsed the ones I had.

"Blister" evidently from the French *blesser*, to wound. A Cajun says, "I kill me three goose and blister one other."

"Plant" evidently like *planter*. When a Cajun says, "I plant me a sticker in my leg," he means, "I got a thorn in my leg."

"Pass out" is used instead of "to go" or "to leave," as "Last night we dance till three o'clock and then pass out."

"Pass for me" means "come by and pick me up."

"Get down" means "come in," evidently a holdover from the horse-and-buggy days.

"Push up" means "move over," as to a person sitting on a couch.

"We are the sixteenth" refers to the date of the month.

"Catch" pronounced ketch, means "fetch." "Ketch me the broom."

"He lives on the pave" meaning "paved road," i.e., highway.

"Pass pleasure" is "Have a good time."

Talk moved from there to Cajun customs and talk. Fred produced from his wallet a business letter from a Cajun that he read aloud to us, and, bless his heart, gave to me. I reproduce it here exactly as it was written.

On Mr. ——:
  Damage roofing job on Blank Street, too remove that big oak lame whitch is broke from the oak tree and fall cross way on the meain roof of the house.
  On this agrement I will remove all the dabree completely out of the lot.

On this agrement I will remove the old roof on all the south side of the house completely out of the lot. I will all so replace all the broken rafters which is on the south side of the house under the broken lem.

On this agrement after I will remove all the old roof all the way on the south side of the house, I will put a new felt on all the south side of the house to match the old. On this questions all the new roof will be 210 compisation too match the old. . . . I will garanteed the roof not any leak from the rain water on my roofing job.

On the north side of that same house I will replace some missing shingle whitch was blowed away from the big storm at the same time when that lem was blowed on the same roofing.

On this agrement on the north side of that same house I cannot garenteeded the north side of the roofing whitch will be a patching roofing job. On this question I can gave a garenteeded on both side of the roofing job if I remove all the old roof out on both side and replace it with new too match the other side roofing job.

On this agrement too do this job as the above explain I will furnish all material to do this roofing job as the above explain and I will all so furnish all the laborint to do this job as the agrement is.

On this agrement when this job will be all complete I will clear the lot another wise I will hall all the dabree completely out of the lot whitch is. . . .

At presient to do this job as the above explain my bid is for the sum of. . . .

I hope my bid will be consider with good consideration. Will be very much appreciated.

Your very trulley

Luncheon itself was what we had come to look upon as a typical Louisiana midday snack; shrimp salad, barbecued chicken, asparagus, rice, candied sweet potatoes and a Bavarian cream for dessert.

Four hours later we were eating again on the same scale at a dinner given for us by Mrs. Frank Gibson at the Gibson farm. There were pleasant people we had not met before and, in addition, our entire group including Rosa, Emma and Clara, and that in itself made a considerable party. Mrs. Dees came, bringing with her two exquisite old luster saucers that she gave to

Darn. Darn was overwhelmed almost into a swound, from which she scarcely emerged all evening.

When drinks were served before dinner, we were asked if we would care to have moose milk, a specialty of the house. I declined but was interested to learn it is made with rum, brandy, bourbon, milk and cream. I do not think Sophy took any but she did make a speech at dinner expressing our gratitude for the generous hospitality that had been extended to us.

Dinner was what in our simpler Northern area of living would be a banquet, but as we were leaving at the end of the evening, Ellen asked if Mrs. Gibson would mind if she took home with her for breakfast some of the fruit from the table decoration. Darn with her cups was not the only one who left with loot.

We went to Little Pecan Island on Saturday, by car close to two hours, and by boat on the bayou and the superb Intercoastal Canal nearly two hours more. We were guests of Mr. Mordelo Vincent, the owner of the island, who goes by plane on weekends to his cottage. He is there in twenty minutes from Lake Charles. I said I preferred four hours on the ground. It was a pleasant day in a strange, far-off place. The Cajun boy in the film *Louisiana Story* lived on Little Pecan, we learned. His family worked for the Vincents. Mr. Vincent told us a photographer from *Life* Magazine came to Little Pecan to photograph the boy and his surroundings, and declared, "Little Pecan is the farthest end of the world," adding that he himself came from New Zealand.

Back at our hotel that night, we said good-by to Emma and Clara on the telephone. I told them our Louisiana party was coming to an end and we were so sad at leaving them we really didn't want to see them; we might weep. They agreed and were tempted they said to come on back to New Orleans with us in order to see us all the way to the end and make sure we saw all the places we ought. Kat, overhearing, said loudly she considered this excessive. Clara came on the telephone. There was one special friend of hers, she told us, we hadn't met and had me write down the address in Natchez, though we weren't going there. We would certainly enjoy him, she was sure. "Of course he's lazy," she explained, "but he's got charm. He was born with a silver spoon in his mouth and never did have the energy to take it out."

I have kept his address. His is an acquaintance I am determined to make.

Ellen, bless her, held us up the following morning. For *once*, I said several times, I was not the one holding up the others. At the very moment of our departure when Sophy was tapping impatient foot signals to get under way, Ellen delayed us. She would like to put on her coat, she said, the air was chillier than she had anticipated in her hotel room. After we had searched the car, removing a considerable amount of baggage, Ellen remembered she'd left the coat hanging in her bedroom closet. She urged us to agree with her how lucky it had been she had wanted to put it on at just that moment.

Returning from her trip upstairs with the coat over her arm, she told us she had decided not to put it on after all. The air seemed a little warmer than she had at first thought, but she would like us to wait a few minutes longer. She had on the return to her hotel room gathered up the fruit remaining there. We might all of us like it on the trip home, she had decided, but had not wanted to delay us by pausing upstairs to wash it. She handed her coat to Sophy to put away in the car, and went back into the lobby where she washed the fruit in a drinking fountain, to the considerable interest of guests sitting nearby and, up to the moment of the diversion she created, reading their Sunday newspapers.

As far as Opelousas we returned by the road on which we had come. We passed a Cajun family on its way to church driving in a two-tiered buggy with a fringed top. A few minutes later passing the church itself, we saw a number of other buggies hitched at the surrounding fence.

We gave ourselves a little time in Opelousas to drive about the town, enjoying some lovely old houses. But once over the Atchafalaya River by way of a Huey Long bridge, we were on a super-highway that ran through swampland and we drove with-

out further stops to Baton Rouge. We lunched there but did not
stop to explore. We visited Afton Villa, however, near St.
Francisville, an early Victorian house of great charm called by
its guide "French Gothic." Admission to this is one dollar and
the house and gardens are well worth seeing. This is one of the
few places in which the interiors have been preserved and restored as well as the house and grounds.

Persuasive signs along the road lead the traveler to believe
Greenwood Plantation is only a step away. It is a step a little akin
to one of Rosa's—thirteen miles out from St. Francisville, nine
miles from the turnoff on Route 61, but it is well worth the
excursion.

We were in New Orleans, back at our old rooms there, in time
for dinner. Dining at Galatoire's, we came at the conclusion of
the meal to a momentous decision: it is both foolish and impossible to say which is the best of the three famous restaurants in
New Orleans, Antoine's, Arnaud's or Galatoire's, and it is equally
foolish to believe there are any better restaurants, anywhere, than
these.

We had pastry and coffee at the little place Sophy had told us
about, Quatres Saisons on St. Peter Street, between Bourbon
and Royal, and talked there of what diets were best, and how
soon one could hope to derive perceptible benefit from any one
of them.

We lunched next day at Antoine's with our dear Howells. It
was a reunion of old friends. And what a lunch—buster crabs for
my companions, oysters Rockefeller for Mrs. Howell, and with
it a card reading this was Oysters Rockefeller No. 1418486. It
was like the ducks at the Tour d'Argent in Paris. For Mr. Howell
and me pompano, as Antoine's cooks it, in a paper bag. We ended
with *café brûlot* as a toast to the Munsons.

From Antoine's we went with the Howells to their apartment
on Royal Street, and at last Mr. Howell fulfilled the promise he
had given to us. We saw the famous and magnificent silver made
from the Mexican silver dollars. By Southern custom we could
not, of course, be in their house without taking refreshment, no

matter how recently and how well we had eaten. We had a liqueur, and this was a specialty of the Howells, one I had not tasted before. We all pronounced it delicious. It is called a Grasshopper, and it is made of one third crème de cacao, one third cream, and one third crème de menthe, beaten lightly and chilled.

When we reluctantly said good-by, Williemel embracing us each in turn, promised if we would come back she would teach us more rules of *bourré* and tell us details she'd left out in the story of her operation.

Our group began to dissolve the following morning. Darn flew to Pasadena, Kat to New York. Ellen, Sophy and I were left to go by train that night. Sophy and I got up early to see first Kat, then Darn on their way. Ellen was a little vexed with us for not calling her because, she explained severely, she was awakened anyway by Kat's getting ready and would have preferred being awake with us to being awake by herself. She breakfasted in the dining room downstairs. Even in that shorter distance than from kitchen up to her bedroom, her egg got too hard. She explained this to Sophy and me when she told us she was going out for a walk by herself. During the day I shopped, of course, buying bunches of vetivert from the Christian Women's Exchange, more perfume, odds and ends. Between purchases I looked again at doorways, patios, grilled galleries, finding some I had not seen before, and I think this can happen to a traveler there on his fiftieth trip. The others were doing much the same things but the three of us did not meet until dinner.

We were packed and immediately we had finished eating at the hotel we separated again temporarily. Ellen and Sophy drove off to Tulane University, where I would join them to hear a concert of the New Orleans Symphony. But first, in a taxi loaded to the roof with our baggage, I went to the station and checked it there. Kat's departure, I realized as I rode, had made no discernible lowering of the original luggage mound.

Sophy and I had been determined from the moment of planning the Louisiana trip to hear our old friend Alex Hilsberg con-

The END

duct the New Orleans Symphony. This was our first opportunity and not easy of accomplishment, because the time of our train departure would come before the end of the program. I raced back in the taxi from the station to the university, joined Sophy, Ellen and Mrs. Hilsberg at the auditorium just before the first number began. We heard beautiful music, sensitively played, and had time to tell this to Alex briefly, in the intermission.

Shortly after the intermission we had to leave. Whispering a good-by to Neya Hilsberg, we scuttled down the aisle and out the building to the curb where the taxi we had ordered was waiting. A gentleman appeared on the sidewalk abreast of us as we were pulling out. I think we had been introduced to him in Alex's dressing room, but in the darkness I could not see his face.

It was his message that startled me. "I wanted to tell you," he said, "if you're not held up by traffic, you ought to get in with a little time to spare. I urge you as the last thing you do, go to —— for a cup of coffee." He named the place to which we had been directed by the bouncer who had ejected us from his restaurant on the night of our arrival in New Orleans.

I daresay I left the gentleman on the curb a little surprised, because there was no time to explain. I put my head out the window as we drove away and called back to him. "This is where we came in." I hope he heard and understood my final message. I said it loud and fervently. "We'll come back."

Behind me, in the cab, Sophy murmured, Ellen joining her, "We certainly will. We certainly will."

Set in Linotype Fairfield
Format by Katharine Sitterly
Manufactured by The Haddon Craftsmen, Inc.
Published by HARPER & BROTHERS, *New York*

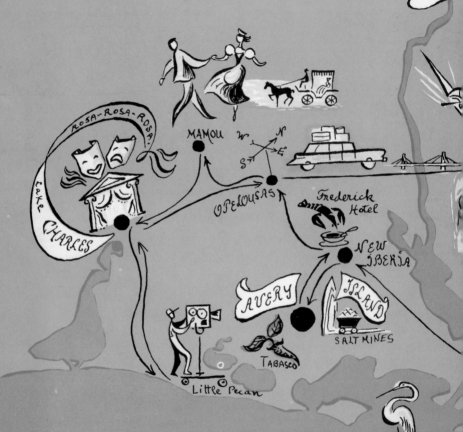

LOUISIANA

ROSA-ROSA-ROSA

Lake CHARLES

MAMOU

OPELOUSAS

Frederick Hotel

NEW IBERIA

AVERY ISLAND

SALT MINES

TABASCO

Little Pecan